The Power of foursquare

7 INNOVATIVE WAYS
TO GET YOUR CUSTOMERS TO
CHECK IN
WHEREVER THEY ARE

Carmine Gallo

New York   Chicago   San Francisco   Lisbon   London   Madrid   Mexico City
Milan   New Delhi   San Juan   Seoul   Singapore   Sydney   Toronto

The McGraw·Hill Companies

1 2 3 4 5 6 7 8 9 10 11 12 13 14 15   QFR/QFR   1 9 8 7 6 5 4 3 2 1

ISBN   978-0-07-177317-1
MHID   0-07-177317-7

e-ISBN 978-0-07-177583-0
e-MHID   0-07-177583-8

Library of Congress Cataloging-in-Publication Data

Gallo, Carmine.
    The power of foursquare : 7 innovative ways to get your customers to check in wherever they are / by Carmine Gallo.
        p.   cm.
        Includes bibliographical references and index.
        ISBN-13: 978-0-07-177317-1 (alk. paper)
        ISBN-10: 0-07-177317-7 (alk. paper)
        1. Internet marketing.   2. Location-based services.   3. Online social networks.   4. Customer relations.   5. Business enterprises—Computer networks.   I. Title.

    HF5415.1265.G35   2012
    658.8'72—dc23   2011025105

Interior design by THINK Book Works

McGraw-Hill books are available at special quantity discounts to use as premiums and sales promotions or for use in corporate training programs. To contact a representative, please e-mail us at bulksales@mcgraw-hill.com.

This book is printed on acid-free paper.

To Vanessa, Josephine, and Lela,
who make my world magical

Contents

Acknowledgments

This book was anything but a solo effort. We included more than 50 case studies of businesses—large and small—that told us their stories, offered insights and tips, and showed us real results from their mobile marketing campaigns. I can't thank all of you enough. Thank you for sharing your stories. Your lessons are invaluable.

Carolyn Kilmer is our Web and community manager at Gallo Communications Group. She spent countless hours tracking down business owners, conducting exclusive interviews, and transcribing conversations. Thanks for all of the wonderful stories you discovered.

Thanks to Pam Condy, our "chief gatekeeper," for coordinating permissions and forms, and keeping us all on track.

My wife, Vanessa, does so much more than manage our business. Her contributions to the book process are invaluable. She helps outline, edit, structure, and make sure we meet our deadlines. She's also an avid foursquare user, and her enthusiasm for the product was contagious.

Special thanks to everyone at foursquare who generously gave us their time. Cofounders Dennis Crowley and Naveen Selvadurai are true entrepreneurs who express themselves with passion, vision, and a deep level of technical knowledge. They are both profoundly inspiring. Foursquare vice president of business development, Tristan Walker, also offered his insights and enthusiasm. Special thanks to foursquare's PR manager, Erin Gleason, for her quick responses to our requests. She is a real professional and a joy to work with.

Foursquare superusers are a unique breed of evangelists. Other than in my research on Apple, I have rarely met a group of customers who exhibit such enthusiasm for a brand. It's been a pleasure to earn your friendship—Dr. Nate Bonilla-Warford, Chad Elkins, Chris Thompson, and Sassy Thomas. Thank you all!

Thanks to my fabulous editor at McGraw-Hill, Gary Krebs. I'm grateful for our collaboration. Marketing whiz Julia Baxter is always a joy to work with, and so is Ann Pryor in PR. I'd also like to thank Lauren Sapira, Lydia Rinaldi, Laura Friedman, and everyone else involved in sales and marketing at McGraw-Hill.

My literary agent, Roger Williams, offers great support and insight. Thank you for your friendship.

My thoughts and prayers go out to Ed Knappman's family. He touched many lives in the publishing industry, including mine. He will always be remembered.

My speaking agent, Tom Neilssen at the BrightSight Group, deserves special thanks for helping me share my content with a wider audience.

Thanks to my family for supporting my efforts and sharing my passion for the subject—Giuseppina, Tino, Donna, Ken, Patty, Francesco, Nick, and my father, who, although he's no longer with us, is always in our lives, shining down on us.

A final shout-out to our friend Tamara Medina for making sure our children were content and happy during the hours we spent researching the book. Now I can fulfill a promise I made to my daughters, who patiently waited for Daddy to finish the book: we're off to Disneyland!

Introduction

What's All the Fuss About?

 *You should be able to stand anywhere in the world, and foursquare will tell you something to do nearby.* "

—**DENNIS CROWLEY,** Cofounder, foursquare

On October 22, 2010, NASA astronaut Douglas Wheelock became the first man to "check in" from space. Back on Earth, 220 miles below, millions of people did the same—at the rate of 23 times *per second*. They checked in to restaurants, bars, stores, hotels, gyms, and other places in every city, country, and continent. What were they doing?

Less than 10 days later, on October 30, 2010, thousands of people pulled out their smartphones and checked in 30,000 times at the Rally to Restore Sanity, hosted by popular "Comedy Central" hosts Jon Stewart and Stephen Colbert. The rally drew 200,000 people to the National Mall in Washington, D.C. It's estimated that 10 percent of those attendees were on foursquare, making it the most checked-in event of 2010. Where were they checking in to?

On December 27, 2010, a massive snowstorm shut down airports and brought travel to a standstill along much of the

1

East Coast, blanketing New York's Central Park under more than 20 inches of snow. More than 10,000 stranded airline passengers and snowbound travelers checked in to a "moving target" venue named Snowpocalypse 2010 and unlocked the rare Epic Swarm badge for doing so. The badge had no practical value except to offer bragging rights—a badge of honor they could share with their friends. That same afternoon, bar owner Alan Cole offered free appetizers to anyone who decided to warm their body and spirit by checking in to his Charlotte, North Carolina, tavern between 4:00 P.M. and 6:00 P.M. Three weeks earlier Cole had started offering incentives for checking in on the tavern's slowest days. His customers didn't receive a badge but were kept quite happy with free potato skins and Al's famous jalapeño poppers. Why were they checking in?

On February 2, 2011, America's favorite groundhog, Punxsutawney Phil, predicted an early spring, and although he emerged from his underground bunker in the Pennsylvania wilds 80 miles northeast of Pittsburgh, 28,000 people around the country shouted, "It's Groundhog Day!" to their foursquare friends, earning the PA Groundhog Day badge for their efforts. Who were all these people, and why were they "shouting" at anyone?

What's all the fuss about?

The fuss, it turns out, is foursquare. Foursquare is a social, location-based service (LBS) smartphone app that makes your world more interesting. People check in on their phones when they arrive at a place, they do so at the rate of two million times a day, and they do so in every country. Five hundred thousand merchants are already using the platform, and the number continues to grow every day. As a local merchant, brand manager, or marketing professional, you'd better know about it, how it works, why it works, and most important, how to make it work for you. Many of your customers are already checking in to your establishment and you might not even know it. We're in the early stages of a fast-growing trend and, with the information in this book, you will be ready to take advantage of this unique opportunity to engage your customers in ways that were never possible before.

Pioneering a Mega Trend in Social Networking: LBS

Foursquare pioneered a megatrend in mobile social networking: location-based services. LBS is not a disease, but it is highly addictive and as a result has the potential to transform conversations—not only between friends, but also between businesses and their customers. By giving the mobile consumer a new, exciting way to explore a city, it offers businesses an extraordinary tool to enhance the relationship with their customers, patrons, and fans.

Foursquare is growing exponentially. It grew 3,400 percent in 2010 over the previous year. Users checked in more than 380 million times during the year and did so in every single country (including North Korea). "We're always surprised,"[1] says foursquare cofounder Dennis Crowley in an exclusive interview for this book. "We started foursquare so 50 of our friends could follow each other around New York City. I recall sitting in an investment meeting and someone asked, 'When are you going to hit one million users?' I said if we ever hit one million users, we've done something right. In one year we hit six million. It's a big surprise."

Even the most optimistic entrepreneur would have been surprised at how quickly foursquare has gained traction among millions of users and evangelists in all parts of the globe. Foursquare launched in March 2009 and grew steadily to one million users by the anniversary of its first year. As more fans acquired a taste for the smartphone app, they spread the word—among their friends and among merchants who would begin to populate and leverage the platform.

In the next three months foursquare had added its next million users. It only took 50 days to grow from four million to five million by November 2010 and only 44 days to reach six

3

Foursquare founders Dennis Crowley and Naveen Selvadurai receive a foursquare Day proclamation from New York City Mayor Michael Bloomberg.

4

million users by January 2011. On a spring Saturday in 2011, foursquare officially "arrived" with an announcement by New York City Mayor Michael Bloomberg, who proclaimed April 16th as "foursquare Day" in the city (see Figure I.1).

Each day 35,000 new users join the international community. Although foursquare was born in New York's East Village, 40 percent of its daily check-ins occur outside the United States. Foursquare is available in multiple languages, including Japanese, Spanish, German, French, Italian, and others.

Millions of people are checking in to every possible location: train stations, hotels, shopping malls, art galleries, concerts, restaurants, bars, movie theaters, gyms, college campuses, and many other venues. Some people are even checking in to cemeteries! Thankfully, these users are very much alive, and you'll learn about them later.

Businesses—large and small—are joining the community. Five months after its launch, only a handful of merchants inquired about joining the platform—about 15 brands in all. Today hundreds of thousands of brands, retailers, and local merchants actively use the platform to reward loyal customers, attract new ones, and engage those customers on a far deeper level than ever before. In addition these businesses are using the platform and accessing a treasure-trove of customer data *for free*. Here is a short list of major well-known brands that have active foursquare partnerships.

- Starbucks
- NASA
- *Wall Street Journal*
- Jimmy Choo
- Chili's Bar & Grill
- Toys"R"Us
- Barnes & Noble
- Bravo
- MTV
- American Express
- History Channel
- RadioShack
- McDonald's
- Sports Authority
- Starwood Hotel and Resorts
- 7-Eleven
- Walmart

5

You'll learn from marketing directors at many of these brands as they share insights into why they're going mobile, results from their campaigns, and tips on how you can do it too. But the real power of foursquare is something already practiced by small, local merchants in every neighborhood in every corner of the planet who offer tips, specials, and rewards to attract new customers, encourage the return of loyal customers, stand out from the competition, and extend their brand.

The Key Questions

Despite foursquare's explosive growth, most merchants have little understanding of just how powerful it can be as a marketing tool. Very few businesses know how best to leverage foursquare to engage their customers. This book is intended to take the mystery out of foursquare and by doing so, help you understand the emerging category of mobile, social, and location-based services. You will hear directly from the top marketing experts in the world. You will learn how large and small companies are using the service to attract, engage, and reward their customers, and you will understand how to successfully implement your own foursquare strategy. You will learn this information through discussions with foursquare's founders, merchants, experts, and the users who love it so much they *volunteer* to support it, build it, and promote it.

I don't pretend to be a social media expert, guru, or ninja. I'm a business owner and a journalist who writes and speaks on the topics of leadership, communications, and innovation. So why would I cover a topic like foursquare? Because it's not just a social media story. It's a communications story, it's an innovation story, and it's fascinating.

Foursquare is a social media tool that businesses of any size can use to tell their stories and engage their customers in an innovative way. I'm not interested in writing a book on how to download the software. You can download the free app and start using it in fewer than two minutes. As a merchant you can claim your venue, create a special, and start reaching your customers in no time—just visit the foursquare website and follow the simple three-step quick guide. As a journalist I'm far more interested in the stories behind the app. There's a story behind every special that a merchant offers. Every badge that someone earns tells a story, as does every tip and every mayorship, all of which you'll be finding out about in the coming pages.

The stories in this book will inspire you. As a business owner or marketer you'll want to hear the story of a struggling restaurant owner who credits foursquare for putting his place on the map. You'll want to read about the government agency that was forced to innovate around mobile networking because it had no advertising budget. You'll want to read about the nonprofit that raised $50,000 for a single campaign, thanks to an innovative check-in strategy. And those stories are just scratching the surface. You'll hear directly from international brands and organizations such as Bravo, the Red Cross, Chili's, RadioShack, Jimmy Choo, and others. You'll hear from small- and medium-sized businesses around the world—hotels, pizza joints, restaurants, bars, wineries, service providers, retail stores, realtors, theme parks, nonprofits, media companies, and colleges. There are more than 50 case studies in this book that will inspire you to look at mobile social networking as an essential component of your growth strategy.

As a journalist I'm also trained to ask questions. You might be asking yourself the same ones: What is it? Why is it important? What's in it for me?

What Is It?

Foursquare is more than just a smartphone application, as you'll see. Users sign up for an account by visiting http://foursquare.com. When they're out and about, they pull out their smartphone and open the foursquare app to see where their friends are or to explore places in their vicinity (e.g., landmarks, stores, restaurants, coffee shops, bars, gyms, and other business and personal establishments). Foursquare will even recommend things to do or places to eat based on a user's check-in history and the check-in trends of their friends. Once they check in by tapping the venue or place name on their phone, they can choose to let friends know where they are and what they are doing. They can also upload a photo, leave tips, or send messages to their friends. They can—and often do— link these activities to Twitter and Facebook. Since it's widely known that word-of-mouth is the most powerful form of advertising, this "sharing" feature is critical for you to understand, appreciate, and leverage.

Also upon checking in, users get points and compete with their friends. They can earn badges for specific check-in behaviors or experiences. They can become the mayor of a venue without ever spending a dime on a campaign—merchants are rewarding them for their loyalty. They can leave tips for any foursquare user who checks in to the same location or a nearby venue. They can get discounts and other rewards from participating local merchants or major brands. They can get free stuff. They can learn more about places they've never visited. Best of all, these users have fun—and they share that fun with friends on their social networks.

One person posted this description of foursquare on Twitter: "Foursquare is a dope little game and you get discounts and free shit if you're the mayor." A little simplified, a little crude perhaps, but that pretty much explains it!

This combination of friend-finder, city guide, and game mechanics creates a highly addictive platform that encourages users to return again and again. It sounds simple, and it is. It's also "insanely addictive" for many people and very powerful.

Here's the truly compelling part, especially for businesses: foursquare turns social networking into a game with its badges and mayorships. This might sound silly to you—and it did to me until I was "ousted" as the mayor of my local coffee shop. *They know my name. They know what I'm going to order before I even reach the counter, and they have my drink prepared for me. I should be the mayor!* (For the record, I did reclaim my rightful position.) People who get ousted as mayors hate getting kicked off their perch. And I mean they get *really* angry. So much so, that they will visit an establishment even more frequently to regain their title. That's powerful!

These mayors love getting rewarded, and the businesses love them right back. Businesses that reward their mayors with a discount or freebies notice a significantly higher level of engagement, sales, and redemptions among their customers—all customers, not just mayors. That's powerful, too! People are more inclined to trust a business if a friend recommends it. If someone who is on your list of foursquare friends posts a tip about a business in your vicinity, it automatically gets pushed to your screen when you're near that establishment. That's powerful indeed—so much so it would be foolish to ignore it.

Why Is It Important?

Foursquare matters, quite simply because people are checking in at the rate of 23 times a second. As smartphones continue to proliferate, the user base is only expected to grow. In 2010, 200 million smartphones were sold around the world. The number is expected to double to 400 million units in 2011, 600 million in 2012, and 700 million in 2013. Foursquare is growing right along with it.

Social networking is no longer a trend—it's mainstream. Mobile social networking is simply the next stage in the evolution of conversations. Facebook has about 150 million active mobile users around the world, which is about as mainstream as it gets. Although foursquare does not have the numbers to match Facebook (yet), it's growing and growing fast, thanks to a swarm of users who are true evangelists. These people get their friends on the platform and bombard local merchants with questions about why they're not being rewarded for being a mayor or a loyal customer. Later in this book, you'll hear from many business owners who adopted foursquare after hearing about it from their customers.

Foursquare keeps adding free tools and features that make it more and more attractive—both to users and merchants. Just days after foursquare launched a new photo-sharing feature, its users were uploading one photo every second (one million photos had been posted in the first three weeks of the service). Foursquare added an Explore tab that suggests things to do, places to eat, and what to see, based on places you've been and the places your friends have visited. Foursquare continues to give merchants more ways to reward loyal customers and merchant tools to analyze the data. Every check-in gives the company—and its partners—a richer

9

set of data points from which to build even more effective campaigns.

These features encourage users to return, and that's why it matters. They come back to unlock specials and promotions, and to earn points, badges, or mayorships. They come back to compete with their friends. They come back to explore their city. Some people love the idea of discovering a city and sharing tips with their friends. For some, they come back to keep a journal of where they've been. Their reasons are different, but they keep coming back. Foursquare's founders will tell you that if you ask 10 different people you will hear 10 different reasons for using foursquare. In short, foursquare has something for everyone, and its growth is staggering.

Foursquare itself might not yet be considered mainstream in a traditional sense, but among its millions of users, it's a daily addiction. As of this writing, 35,000 new users are joining the platform *every single day*—more than one million *each month*. It matters to them, and so it should matter to you. These users are waiting for you to engage them.

More than 100 local user communities around the globe only want to promote the service and to connect like-minded fans. It matters to them. There is a story behind every badge, and you will hear directly from users who share their stories—it matters to them. Since foursquare is an open API (application programming interface), thousands of developers are building services to complement the site. Today you can download foursquare to your iPhone, BlackBerry, Android, or other device. But it didn't start that way. For example, foursquare's team was not the first to develop an Android app. Third-party programmers built it, and foursquare then took it in-house to improve it—but developers built it first.

Foursquare does not have an army of salespeople making cold calls to sign up merchants. Why? Because they don't have to. Their users do it for them. Foursquare even started an ambassador program for superusers passionate about the company. These evangelists were asked to fill out a form on the foursquare website; if approved, they received a pack of foursquare Ambassador cards (custom-printed with their names). They handed out these cards to local businesses to encourage them to sign up and offer specials. The ambassadors did not get paid. They did it because they love foursquare.

Many brands are leveraging the platform to engage their customers. They are not waiting for case studies. They *are* the case studies. Some analysts are predicting that local and social mobile tools will revolutionize the way commerce is done, and they are singling out foursquare as one of the most important new marketing tools to engage your customers and grow your business. If you're looking for a metric that measures your return on investment (ROI), you'll find it among the brands featured in this book (although the "investment" is near zero). But if you consider the fact that not all impact takes the form of purely financial metrics, you will find that foursquare offers even more powerful forms of impact: engagement, awareness, influence, and loyalty.

Cofounders Dennis Crowley and Naveen Selvadurai started the business by asking themselves one question: how do you turn life into a game? The answer was to get rewarded for seeking out new experiences.

By combining game mechanics and GPS-enabled smartphones, this team made it so that local merchants and business owners can connect with their customers in ways that are far more interesting than ever before. Merchants can reach their customers wherever they are, in front of a computer, on the go, or even in a competitor's location.

Mobile communication, social networking tools, and geolocation services are not going away anytime soon. On the contrary, with the advent of faster cell phone networks and the explosive growth in the smartphone market, mobile social networking is only bound to grow, becoming essential to how people live their daily lives. Sixty percent of all mobile Internet usage is now spent on social networking sites like Facebook and Twitter. And as you'll learn, these social networks complement foursquare and help unlock its full power and potential.

People use mobile social media to connect—with friends, brands, merchants, and a broader social network. Mobile social networking plays a powerful role in people's lives because it acts as an intrinsic and extrinsic motivator:

Intrinsic	Extrinsic
build self-esteem	receive rewards
gain meaning to life	collect badges
establish a feeling of importance	get discounts
satisfy curiosity	earn points
experience the joy of learning, discovery, and sharing	win free stuff

What's in It for Me?

Ah, the ultimate question. For users, foursquare simply makes their lives more interesting and fun. What could be more of an incentive than that? Foursquare enhances people's life experiences. Is it a mobile app that everyone needs? Nope. But it makes users' lives more entertaining. By doing so it can help a brand, retailer, or local merchant attract new customers, engage a higher level of loyalty, and give the brand top-of-mind status. For marketers and business owners, foursquare is a tool that you can use to extend your brand story as well to gain a variety of ways to attract, retain, reward, and engage your customers. With fourquare you can do the following:

- Reward your best customers.
- Create specials that attract people who are near your venue but not in it.
- Offer valuable tips, insights, and information.
- Get free access to data, real-time statistics, and customer analytics that small businesses have never had easy access to until now.

In the pages that follow, I'll give you plenty of reasons why you should care about foursquare and the booming growth in LBS. You'll read about dozens of companies that are finding success with it and, hopefully, be inspired to experiment with your own campaign. Some of the merchants, businesses, and major brands who tell their stories include:

- a boutique hotel that credits foursquare for helping it compete against larger, more established chains
- a matchmaker who owes her entire business to foursquare
- a popular chain of ice cream parlors that has seen a sizable increase in business since launching a foursquare campaign
- a major university that embraces foursquare to engage its students, donors, and visitors
- a national television network that is using foursquare to market its programs and to extend its brand
- a nonprofit organization that has raised $50,000 for an environmental campaign solely by using foursquare
- a Milwaukee restaurant that has attracted 150 regular and new customers on one slow night thanks to foursquare and has since embraced foursquare to make it one of the most popular restaurants in town

Before you dive in and learn more, I'm going to give you three final reasons why you should care right now. First, it's free. You have nothing to lose. Second, your customers are probably already using it. Third, the growth story is unquestionably impressive and you will want to be a part of it.

Before foursquare reached its second anniversary, it had recorded more than 250 million check-ins from users worldwide. Its appeal is international. Tokyo was one of the most checked-in cities even before the localized version of the application became available. In fewer than two years, foursquare topped 6 million users. Today it's more than 10 million users. It's growing faster than Twitter did at similar stages. So again, what's in it for you? It's free, it's growing like crazy, and your customers are already using it. Go get them.

When I began researching this book, I asked myself a question you might be asking yourself right now: What type of businesses should use foursquare? The answer surprised me:

CHECKING IN

FOURSQUARE USER GROWTH HISTORY

- **March 13, 2009:** launched at the popular social media conference South by Southwest
- **April 22, 2010:** hit 1 million registered users
- **August 22, 2010:** hit 3 million users
- **December 1, 2010:** hit 5 million users, prompting a flurry of press activity
- **January 14, 2011:** hit 6 million users (growth obtained faster than anyone—themselves included—had predicted)
- **Today:** more than 10 million users as of this writing and growing exponentially!

just about anyone. Big brands are actively using foursquare, and you will hear directly from many of them in the pages to follow: brands like Bravo, NASA, Chili's, the American Red Cross, Starbucks, and many others. Media properties use foursquare. Retailers use foursquare. Restaurants use foursquare. Business-to-consumer brands use it, as do business-to-business firms. Service brands use it. Realtors use it, as do consultants, entrepreneurs, and small business owners. Wineries use it, as do pizza chains and sandwich shops. Foursquare applies to everyone.

The devastating global recession has forced businesses to develop innovative ways of engaging their customers. Average simply doesn't cut it anymore for companies competing in a brutally competitive global economy. Being average only guarantees below-average results. We are now entering the age of "extra": extra quality, extra skills, and extra services to engage your customers. Foursquare could be the extra you need to launch and grow a successful business.

Seven Keys to Unlock Your Business Potential

After extensive interviews with foursquare's founders, investors, customers, fans, partners, social media, and marketing experts, I have discovered seven big ideas that will help you CHECK IN to the power of foursquare to unlock your brand's potential:

(C)onnect Your Brand. Align your foursquare strategy with your brand's value proposition and your brand story.

(H)arness New Fans. Use foursquare to attract new customers who otherwise might not know about your business or who don't keep it top of mind.

(E)ngage Your Followers. Add insights and information to keep your brand in front of your customers and fans wherever they are.

(C)reate Rewards. Leverage foursquare's powerful and free tools to learn more about your best customers and to create rewards for their loyalty.

(K)nock Out the Competition. Outsmart your competitors by being a leader in this new space and develop creative campaigns. Don't wait for case studies—be the case study.

(I)ncentivize Your Customers. Give your customers a reason to check in, again and again.

(N)ever Stop Entertaining. Foursquare is a playful platform. Always have fun.

15

Each idea in C-H-E-C-K-I-N is featured in its own chapter. Following each of these chapters are supporting chapters that feature two specific case studies reinforcing the big ideas. The titles of each supporting chapter are coined from the names of some popular foursquare badges.

Facebook started as a way for friends to connect online, much as foursquare started as a way for a group of friends to find each other in a big city. Facebook began with a few thousand users in a New England college and grew to 500 million fans around the world. Foursquare is following a similar trajectory. Major brands that established an early presence on Facebook struggled at the beginning. Coca-Cola had 800 Facebook fans in November 2007. Today it has 16.5 million. Early leaders were rewarded. Those brands that are experimenting with LBS tools like foursquare might end up being light-years ahead of their competitors as the platform gains popularity. There are always business owners, entrepreneurs, and managers who will wait to see how others do it. Do it first.

If someone asks you what foursquare is, you would be entirely correct to use any of these answers:

- It's a social, local, and mobile networking tool.
- It's a location-based social network.
- It's a geolocation app.
- It's a game.
- It's a communications tool.
- It's a new social-media marketing platform.

These examples answer the question, "What is it?" But for marketers or business owners, it's more instructive to ask, "What does it stand for?"

Simply put, foursquare is a tool that helps you explore your world. It illuminates, informs, and inspires. It invites us to experiment, share, and have deeper, more meaningful conversations with friends and the brands that touch our lives.

CHAPTER 1

Connect Your Brand

"We are constantly surprised by what our partners are doing and how users are extending the platform in ways that we never expected."

—NAVEEN SELVADURAI, Cofounder, foursquare

ew Yorkers who are in a hurry for lunch know better than to drop by the Shake Shack at Madison Square Park in Chelsea. Yes, the burger joint offers some of the best hot dogs, fries, custards, and high-grade Black Angus beef burgers in the city, but people have to wait—and wait—for it. Between the hours of 12:00 noon and 2:00 P.M., a hungry customer can easily be kept waiting for 35 minutes or longer. In the summer the line can stretch to an hour.

How should customers spend this time? Sure, they can check their e-mail, make a call, or strike up a conversation with the person next to them. Here's another idea: when standing in the Shake Shack line at Madison Green, look up to see a number of life-size cast-iron sculptures of artist Anthony Gormley's body standing on buildings that surround the park. I don't live in New York, nor have I ever visited the neighborhood before, so how did I learn about this piece of trivia when I ate at the Shake Shack for the first time? The Corcoran Group told me—on foursquare.

The Corcoran Group is the largest residential real estate firm in New York City. The company was founded in 1973 as New York City was beginning a historic transition from being predominantly a rental market to one of individual ownership. Today Corcoran's 2,000 agents generate more than $18 billion in sales annually. The Corcoran Group embraces the spirit of innovation, and social media is just the latest tool in its arsenal.

Corcoran doesn't wait for others to lead the way, especially when it comes to social networking tools that allow its realtors to form deeper and longer-lasting relationships with prospects and clients. As early as 1995, The Corcoran Group launched one of the first real estate websites, www.corcoran

.com. Today it attracts more than four million visitors per month and produces more sales than any other website in residential real estate.

In December 2009, Corcoran introduced an iPhone app. Instead of looking through the Sunday newspaper for listings, a young couple having brunch in the East Village can simply open the app to see properties for rent or for sale in the area. It also provides more details about the listing. Corcoran thinks of it as a wonderful open-house tool. But when foursquare entered the picture, it changed everything. Corcoran had always been in the "location" business; now it had the opportunity of putting the full range of its unique expertise right into the hands of its customers, wherever they happen to be in the city.

A Powerful Marketing Proposition

Corcoran is a company rooted in the location business. Its agents pride themselves on sharing localized knowledge of the city's neighborhoods. "The core mission of the Corcoran brand is to communicate what it's like to live in an area. It goes beyond the four walls of an apartment to include what's nearby. This is where foursquare becomes a great marketing fit,"[1] says Corcoran director of interactive product and marketing Matthew Shadbolt. "It's an extension of what we do offline. It allows us to share local tips specific to venues that are directly around a client wherever they are in the city. For example, we can tell you what to order at a particular restaurant, how to get into a club, or where to sit on the subway. We put Corcoran expertise in your hands as you explore the city. That's a very powerful marketing proposition."

Here's how it works. Open the foursquare app anywhere in Manhattan, Brooklyn, the Hamptons, or Palm Beach, Florida, and it's nearly impossible to avoid Corcoran's tips—inside information and recommendations about local venues. These tips are available for any foursquare user to see. If you "follow" Corcoran on foursquare—as more than 10,000 people

19

have chosen to do— its tips get automatically pushed to your phone when you check in to a location where Corcoran has left a recommendation or suggestion. It's like getting a recommendation from a trusted friend. Corcoran has created more than 1,500 tips for venues in most every neighborhood in its territory:

- **Apple Store (401 W. 14th):** You can't leave Chelsea without a stop off at the Apple store at 14th Street and 9th Avenue, a beautiful three-story loft building with a sexy glass curtain covering it.
- **Manhattan Mall (100 W. 33rd):** Use the mall to cut through between Penn Station and the 34th Street subway stations when it's raining.
- **Denino's Pizzeria Tavern (524 Port Richmond Ave., Staten Island):** Old-school joint serving some of the best pizza in all five boroughs. Start with an order of wings or fried calamari, and then move onto the Garbage Pie.

20

Since Shadbolt and his interactive product and marketing team are the ones populating the Corcoran foursquare site with tips, they can add tips every week as they visit new restaurants, bars, stores, or other neighborhood venues. Foursquare isn't static for Corcoran. It's not an app that they create once and let go. It's a constantly evolving program to meet the needs of Corcoran's clients.

Foursquare allows anyone to leave tips for a particular venue, and those tips are displayed on a user's page in two categories: recent and popular. This free data gives Shadbolt the kind of information he can use to refine Corcoran's tips. For example, Shadbolt has noticed that the most popular tips are accessed in venues where people are expected to wait in lines: train stations, popular restaurants, movie theaters, and yes, the Shake Shack. Based on this insight, Shadbolt adds more tips to these types of venues. Here are some of the more popular Corcoran tips you'll find as you explore New York City:

- **Magnolia Bakery (401 Bleeker Street):** Legendary cup-cakes. Absolutely get the Red Velvets! Well worth standing in line for this New York classic.
- **Eataly (5th and 23rd):** Go right when they open, to avoid the crowds and get the best selection. Otherwise, you'll be forced to wait in line outside.
- **Good Enough to Eat (483 Amsterdam):** The biscuits and strawberry butter make this place the best brunch on the Upper West Side.
- **21 Club (21 W. 53rd):** The key to power lunching is landing the right table. The left section of the dining room is pre-ferred, and the right, known as "Siberia" to its regulars, is by no means coveted.
- **The Lincoln Center Fountain (Columbus Avenue and 64th):** The fountain cycles through a water show every hour, but beware if you're sitting on the marble edges as the water shoots up very fast and you can (and will) get wet!

Align foursquare with Your Core Mission

The Corcoran Group is not interested in offering badges, specials, or other deals (more on these later). They are not interested in rewarding mayors. They are not interested in giving foursquare users a 10 percent discount for checking in to an apartment (although 10 percent off a million-dollar NYC apartment would be very cool). Deals, specials, and rewards are not aligned with Corcoran's core mission. The Corcoran Group is in the business of selling homes by offering enhanced client services: services that set it apart from other real estate firms. Localized knowledge is at the center of that experience.

"One of the main reasons we're on foursquare is because it's a personalized and powerful form of marketing. A ban-ner ad on the desktop might generate a visitor who stays on our site for a few seconds and leaves. But if someone is new to the city or a neighborhood, eats at a restaurant they've never been to, reads our tip about what to order from the menu, and shares that tip with friends, that's a much more powerful form of marketing,"[2] says Shadbolt. "Foursquare is an extension of our brand in a fun, helpful, and incredibly targeted way."

Reread that last sentence. Foursquare is an "extension" of the Corcoran brand. It doesn't replace agents. It complements the work they already do. Corcoran's product is the physical property for sale or rent, but the brand stands for localized neighborhood expertise. This has been what Corcoran agents have always stood for—knowing the neighborhood better than anyone else and sharing a deep level of knowledge about what it's like to live in a particular area. Foursquare simply allows the brand to extend that conversation and to engage in a digital dialogue with a new and growing base of users.

One foursquare user in Palm Beach was having dinner with friends and decided to look up tips left by other foursquare users. Corcoran had populated nearby venues with tips, including the restaurant where the man was enjoying his time with friends. He used a Corcoran tip to order the meal and enjoyed the fact that a real estate agency was sharing local knowledge. The man happened to be in the home-buying process and the next day called the local Corcoran office to set up an appointment. Two days later he was viewing properties. According to Shadbolt, "We gave this person a valuable lifestyle experience. That's a powerful form of marketing. It's more powerful in my opinion than classified ads, banner ads, or search advertising." That's the power of foursquare.

Valuable Tips for Snowbound Realtors

Shadbolt thinks creatively about aligning the foursquare platform with the Corcoran mission. One of his most effective campaigns didn't cost a dime, except for the cost of a few hours of time. From January 12–14, 2011, thousands of real estate professionals converged on the Marriott Marquis in NYC's Times Square for the semiannual Real Estate Connect conference to learn about emerging trends in technology and real estate. Shadbolt knew it would be snowing that week and that meant thousands of real estate professionals (brokers, agents, executives) would be searching for places to eat nearby. He also knew that hundreds, if not thousands, of the attendees would be foursquare users. He turned out to be right on both counts.

Shadbolt's innovative idea was to place tips for popular venues within a 10-block radius of the Marriott. Here are some examples of the Corcoran tips realtors discovered when they checked in to foursquare:

- **Aureole (three blocks away on One Bryant Park):** An exceptional pre-theater prix fixe deal—try the crab soup and the flatiron steak! Or go after theater for the Bubbles After Broadway.
- **Café Edison (four blocks away on Broadway and 8th):** Great place for lunch with one of the best matzo ball soups in the city. The French fries and the split pea soup aren't bad either!
- **Victor's Café 52 (seven blocks away on Broadway and 8th):** Awesome atmosphere and aromas from this delicious Cuban joint. Try the not-so-cheap pitcher of sangria and the lobster empanadas.

During the conference week, Corcoran saw a "marked increase" in the tips that had been posted for venues in the 10-block radius. Each day of the conference, attendees would tell Shadbolt and other Corcoran employees that they had seen and used their recommendations. It left an impression and stamped the brand on the minds of the attendees. According to Shadbolt, "Now they know that when they come to New York, they should look to Corcoran for advice. That's a very powerful brand play. If you want to know anything about what it's like to live in New York City, it stamps us as the ones with the most specialized knowledge. We get name recognition and much, much more. It shows that we offer a level of customer services that exceeds their expectations."

CHECKING IN

"At Corcoran we cannot share local neighborhood expertise on a desktop as effectively as we can in the palm of your hand. Foursquare is a perfect tip because it solves a problem: How to get Corcoran expertise into people's hands wherever they are in the city? Use foursquare to solve problems."

—MATTHEW SHADBOLT,
Director of Internet Marketing, the Corcoran Group

Remember that the businesses most likely to succeed in the next decade are those that offer something extra. Corcoran has always been in the business of extra service. Foursquare simply allows Corcoran to extend that brand promise. As Shadbolt says, "That's powerful."

The Most Important Question to Ask

Before deciding to launch a foursquare strategy or figuring out how to leverage foursquare to engage your customers, you need to ask yourself a very important question: What business am I in? This question should elicit a far different answer than the question: What does my business do? For example, Corcoran sells real estate. That's what the business does. But that's not what business they are in. They are in the business of providing unmatched localized knowledge.

Let me explain. I actually learned the difference between these two questions from Starbucks founder and CEO Howard Schultz. We were talking one day, and I mentioned that he rarely uses the word *coffee* in his conversations. Schultz says coffee is what they sell as a product, but it's not the business he's in. Starbucks, he explained, stands for much more than coffee: exceptional customer service, happy employees, and an experience "between work and home." The product— coffee— is a means to the end. (Starbucks was also the first major chain to offer a customized badge on foursquare. More on badges later.)

Let me ask you the same question that Schultz posed: What business are you in? This question is critical to building a creative and successful foursquare strategy. No social media campaign on Facebook, Twitter, or foursquare stands a chance of success if it is not connected, or aligned, with your brand story. And everyone has a story to tell, especially a 100-year-old hotel.

How a Start-Up Helped a Century-Old Hotel

Many people recognize the Algonquin Hotel in New York for its famed Oak Room, where dark paneled walls, white table-cloths, and a gleaming piano conjure up a supper club from a more glamorous era. The Oak Room was a launching pad for Harry Connick, Jr., Michael Feinstein, Diana Krall, and many others. Entertainment plays a leading role in the hotel's historical brand story—at 100 years of age, the Algonquin is New York City's oldest operating hotel and has been designated as a New York City landmark. But how can a hotel steeped in such rich history leverage a service that, at the time, had yet to reach its second anniversary? Unlike Corcoran, the Algonquin has a physical venue so it can offer a discount, such as "Get 50 percent off any Tonic & Tomes at the Blue Bar for checking in. Get a free appetizer from the bar menu if you're the mayor" (more on specials later).

But the Algonquin wanted to use foursquare to offer more than a rate, a room, and a discount. It wanted to be involved in the conversations that people had about the city. As a famed gathering spot for New York's cultural and artistic elite for 100 years, the Algonquin knows a thing or two about the city. So the Algonquin's marketing agency, The Zimmerman Group, decided to extend the hotel's history and expertise to a new and growing demographic of mobile urban professionals. The decision was made to team up with foursquare to give users the inside scoop on what to do when they visited the city. Here are some sample foursquare tips left by the Algonquin:

- **Rockefeller Center:** Go to Midtown at 7 A.M. to see the "Today Show" being taped or get there early, claim your space in the southeast corner behind the anchor's desk, and get tapped to be on live TV yourself.
- **Empire State Building:** Both the Empire State Building (ESB) and the Algonquin are deeply rooted in NYC history. The ESB was named a historic monument in 1986, just a year before the Algonquin.
- **Diamond District:** This is where 90 percent of diamonds entering the country begin their journey. Some end up nearby in a martini served on the world's hardest $10,000 rocks for added charm at the Algonquin.

By populating foursquare with tips about NYC's most historic places, the Algonquin becomes more than just a nice place to rest your head. The Algonquin decided that its foursquare strategy would be to extend its expertise to the entire city, helping visitors explore the city whether they were staying at the hotel or not.

A Check-In to Die For

Less than one mile from the heart of downtown Atlanta sits the final resting place for many of the area's settlers, builders, and noted citizens. Maynard Jackson, Atlanta's first African American mayor, is buried there, as is Margaret Mitchell, author of *Gone with the Wind*. Founded in 1850, the Oakland Cemetery is a popular destination for visitors who take both self-paced and guided tours. The cemetery even offers a tour on Halloween night for the truly courageous. But that's not all. Oakland Cemetery offers its visitors a foursquare special. Every person who purchases a guided tour and checks in using foursquare gets a free soda or bottled water, 25 percent off a self-guided tour map, and 10 percent off all purchases at the gift shop.

The special was created by Chad Elkins, a superuser who founded Foursquare Atlanta, a community of users who share foursquare news, promote local events, and offer customer support. (Elkins is not compensated for this work. He does it because he loves it and wants to spread the word about foursquare. Again, these are powerful supporters to have in your corner.) Elkins also volunteers as a tour guide for the historical cemetery. He wanted to create a mobile social presence for the cemetery because it was off the beaten path. Many Atlanta tourists will visit the Atlanta History Museum or the Georgia Aquarium without appreciating the hidden treasure just a mile from downtown Atlanta, a showplace of sculpture, nature, architecture, and history.

The Oakland Cemetery's foursquare special is perfectly consistent with its marketing goals: to attract paying visitors, to promote events (it hosts musical acts), and to make people feel more comfortable about calling Oakland a "permanent" home. Oakland isn't alone. It's not uncommon to find cemetery directors creating more events to attract customers. And there's a reason for it. As more Americans opt for cremations, demand for burial plots has slackened. Some superintendents say they have to lighten up their image. Events, tours, art, and music are just some ways cemeteries are striving to improve their image. By adding foursquare to the mix, the Oakland Cemetery has truly created a marketing campaign to die for.

History Comes Alive on foursquare

How did I learn that the Oakland Cemetery is Atlanta's oldest cemetery or that it is the final resting place for many of the area's historically famous citizens? A Google search didn't teach me. The History Channel did on foursquare. In fact, it's one of the most popular tips accessed by foursquare users who visit the cemetery.

History partnered with foursquare in conjunction with a 12-hour television event called "America, The Story of Us." The program told the 400-year story of America—its people, places, and events that shaped the nation. The cable network not only managed to integrate a foursquare campaign with its mission—bringing history alive—but also used the campaign to create buzz for an exciting new series. Along the way it realized that its historical tips and unusual insights could help foursquare users unlock the history in their cities. The more tips that users discovered led them one step closer to unlocking a custom History badge as well.

The campaign worked like this: when a foursquare user checked into a city, if the user was near a location featured in the "America" series or another historical location, he or she would find trivia and information created by History (formerly known as the History Channel). For example, on a recent flight from the San Francisco Bay area to San Diego, I opened foursquare as soon as we landed so I could check in to the airport. Now keep in mind that I am "following" History. It's like following a friend, but in this case my "friend" is a brand. Remember if your friends leave a tip, those tips get automatically pushed to your phone when you check in to the same place. So I landed, opened foursquare, checked in, and was greeted with this piece of trivia: Since you're at the San Diego International Airport (SAN): SAN, dedicated in 1928, is also known as Lindbergh Field. San Diego was the city from which Charles Lindbergh began the journey that would become the first solo transatlantic flight (see Figure 1.1).

History has left more than 1,000 tips and historical insights in unique places around the country. A foursquare visitor to New York's St. Paul's Chapel will learn that George Washington worshipped there in 1789. Thousands of foursquare visitors who have checked into the Magic Kingdom in Lake Buena Vista, Florida, are learning that the park opened in 1971 and is the world's largest and most visited recreational resort, and that Walt Disney passed away before Disney

FIGURE 1.1

A History Channel and foursquare campaign provided followers with location-based trivia.

World was completed. When my family stayed at the Bellagio Hotel in Las Vegas, History had information for us, too. We learned that it was the most expensive hotel ever built when it opened in 1998 ($1.6 billion). Farther west, in Coronado, California, I learned that the historic Hotel Coronado was built in 1888 and that it was the first hotel in the world to use electrical lighting. History also offered me some good advice—Rooms 3502 and 3327 are reported to be haunted! Good thing the conference I was attending had blocked off rooms in another section.

History's foursquare campaign acts as an extension of the channel's unique content, reaching viewers even when they are not on the couch watching the network. If you review the questions asked earlier, History might answer them like this: What do you do? We operate a television network. What business are you in? We unlock the history in your city.

Unlocking a city is perfectly aligned with foursquare's mission to help users discover their cities. According to foursquare cofounder Naveen Selvadurai, foursquare is different than other social media networks because it encourages you to get away from your computer screen and explore the world around you. "We started the service in a playful way to make cities easier to explore. Everyone—young and old—can fall in love with it. We want to get people to try new things, explore their city, and share that experience with friends."[3]

USA Today *Keeps Up with Changing Habits*

Using foursquare to leave tips seems perfectly aligned with brands offering content of any type. As you would expect, publishers have eagerly embraced the platform. From the *Wall Street Journal* to *USA Today*, major content providers are leveraging foursquare to extend their unique content to a younger, mobile demographic.

Foursquare is a natural fit for publishers who are struggling to find new ways of leveraging their expertise—content—with the changing habits of today's readers. *USA Today* launched its foursquare partnership in January 2011. The newspaper populated its account with 250 tips from its travel experts and writers. The advice extends the reach of its popular feature "10 Great Places," which taps local experts, authors, and celebrities for exclusive insider scoops on top destinations. For example, visitors to San Francisco are advised to check out the Castro Theater's "rollicking sing-along nights" while gamblers in Las Vegas are told that the showgirl statues at the Riviera Hotel and Casino might bring them luck. Travelers who prefer a quieter trip are encouraged to visit the Biltmore Estate in Asheville, North Carolina, or the orchid conservatory in Atlanta's Botanical Garden.

Think about where people read *USA Today*. It's the number one newspaper at hotels, often waiting outside your door in the morning. It's read on airplanes, in lobbies, and in resort destinations. It's a traveler's companion. Foursquare is an extension of that role, helping users find undiscovered points of interest or quality attractions as they travel. *USA Today* provides a wealth of content for travelers. Foursquare's promise is to help you explore your city. As such it acts as a brand extension. It's a natural fit.

China Checks In

With a print circulation of about 400,000, *China Daily* sells newspapers. But as the leading English-language newspaper in China, its mission is to promote China and its innovations to the English-speaking world. *China Daily*'s mission is to "promote constructive dialogue between China and the United States."[4] Its foursquare strategy is perfectly consistent with this mission. According to its foursquare venue page, *China Daily* "would like to take you to almost every corner of China and help you explore the mysteries of the oriental country."

Foursquare users who are near the Victoria and Albert Museum in Beijing might want to pay the museum a visit after learning that magnificent imperial robes from 1644 to 1911 are part of the display. According to *China Daily*'s foursquare tips, the robes are part of the treasured collections of the Palace Museum. Visitors to the Yunnan Province might learn that there is a deep canyon nicknamed the Tiger Leaping Gorge. According to *China Daily*, the name comes from a legend about a tiger that once jumped across the gorge at its narrowest section. With a drop of 3,000 meters, the gorge is believed to be one of the world's deepest canyons. And, of course, if you're anywhere near the Great Wall you will learn that "Norwegian Robert Loken spent 601 days walking across the Great Wall. He started from Jiayuguan and

31

CHECKING IN

"Before you decide on creative ways to use foursquare for your business, set up a personal account and start using it yourself. See it through your customers' eyes first."[5]

—CHRIS THOMPSON,
Blogger, About Foursquare (http://aboutfoursquare.com)

reached the final eastern watchtower in Liaoning's Hushan on December 2." [6]

China Daily's posts are updated regularly with museum exhibits, art shows, seasonal tourist attractions, and more. *China Daily* does not use foursquare to overtly sell newspapers, but by delivering its unique expertise to English-speaking smartphone users wherever they are in the country, the newspaper connects its content with thousands of potential subscribers.

Time Out *for Tips*

Time Out New York is a magazine famous for its offbeat lists of restaurants, nightlife, and activities. It's also wildly popular and one of the leading periodicals in the United States, right behind the *Economist* in terms of advertising pages. City-specific *Time Out* magazines can also be found in Chicago, Boston, London, and Sydney, among other cities. *Time Out* is a leading arts and entertainment guide for these cities, but the New York issue leads the pack.

Readers of *Time Out New York* can check out its listings to find ideas for the best movie theater for date night, 50 things to do under $5, or best hook-up bars. Every week they can find a popular feature called "Things to Do," which highlights the 15 best things to do in the city for the week.

Foursquare is nicely aligned with *Time Out New York*'s demographic—young, active, and influential. Since these readers are also increasingly mobile, *Time Out New York* decided to use tips to reach these people wherever they happened to be in the city. Here are some *Time Out New York* tips a foursquare user might find in New York City:

- ◆ **Village Pourhouse (64 3rd Avenue):** Tuesday nights here are devoted to Rock Band with drink specials like the $5 rum-based Pourhouse Punch and the occasional open bar.
- ◆ **Brooklyn Botanical Garden (Brooklyn, NY):** Take in the beautiful foliage, and treat yourself to ice cream at the café. In

winter when it's too cold to stroll, visit the climate-controlled Steinhardt Conservatory.

+ **City Bakery (3 W. 18th Street):** Must try—the incredibly rich hot chocolate with fat, house-made marshmallows and the most melted chocolate-chip cookies.

Time Out New York doesn't get a cut of the business from sending their readers to any of these venues, but if you are one of their 20,000 foursquare followers, the magazine is delivering its expertise right to the palm of your hand, wherever you are in the city.

Foursquare users who visit four of *Time Out New York*'s recommended venues will get something extra special—*Time Out New York*'s Happy Hour badge. Now here's where things get interesting. On any given day, some of the people who unlock the badge will choose to share the information with their Twitter and Facebook followers. This represents an additional layer of free promotion for the magazine. For example, in one 24-hour period, I counted 35 people who had unlocked the badge and linked their foursquare check-ins to Twitter (many more had unlocked the badge, but about 25 percent of users choose to connect to another social network). By sharing their badge achievement with their friends and followers, these Twitter posts are being shared with tens of thousands of additional people. The math is pretty easy to follow. Each and every day, seven days a week, 52 weeks a year, *Time Out New York*'s brand is being shared and recognized by far more people than just those who pick up the weekly magazine. That's smart.

Singapore's King of Beer

Fun, interesting, and timely content goes hand-in-hand with foursquare tips. But while content is king for many brands, beer might be the chaser for you. It's free and easy for anyone—a user or a business—to provide tips on foursquare. It's also free and easy for local merchants to offer customized foursquare specials to their customers and reward their most loyal patrons.

You will learn a lot more about specials and rewards in the following chapters, but for now, keep in mind that depending on your business, offering specials to your customers might be more aligned with your product and foursquare's users than leaving tips.

Singapore is home to an award-winning microbrewery called Brewerkz. The restaurant offers burgers, juicy ribs, and wood-fired pizzas, all in hearty "American portions." When the restaurant first started, founder Devin Kimble found a niche—he discovered that people in Singapore were craving a really good burger, so he started an American-style restaurant, catering to the large expat community in the region. Today they have broadened their appeal, and while the food is a draw, patrons go mostly for the wide selection of handcrafted beer. The owners of Brewerkz created a tiered foursquare special. Anyone who checks in and adds a tip receives free fries. But the mayor gets something extra special—one free pint of beer with any purchase. The mayor gets a free pint on each day he or she retains the title. This tiered strategy accomplished two things: First, by connecting a check-in special to a tip, Brewerkz attracted about 300 tips to its venue page and nearly 5,000 check-ins. Second, it helped spread the word about the restaurant's most tempting creation—handcrafted beer.

The folks who own Brewerkz understand the power of foursquare to build a strong local presence. Not only is their foursquare strategy consistent with their product, it is a complement to their existing social media dialogue with customers. Brewerkz maintains its own Twitter account (@BrewerkzSG), which it uses frequently. What could a beer joint tweet about? Plenty. Brewerkz uses Twitter to announce promotions, events, and tweetup invites. It discusses the launch of new beers with trivia and interesting facts. It also runs contests, like on the day it launched a new dragon fruit and honey beer and asked Twitter followers to name it. It's also on

Facebook. When Brewerkz started its Facebook page, it offered its first 1,000 fans free beer. It worked better than expected. The page has gathered 3,000 fans and continues to grow.

As Brewerkz proves, foursquare doesn't replace Twitter and Facebook, but it allows the restaurant to reach out to its customers and reward them for their patronage—making a connection with those customers that it may not have done otherwise. It also allows Brewerkz to remain on the cutting edge of social technology and brings a sense of fun and excitement to its customers. As you will hear from other brands, retailers, and local merchants, foursquare complements those two popular social networking sites quite nicely. While the three social networking sites are independent tools, a brand can use them together to communicate a seamless, consistent, and compelling story.

 UNLOCK THE POWER   35

◆ **Join the community.** Before you engage your customers on foursquare, take time to understand the service by participating. Visit http://foursquare.com, click the "Join Now" button, create a personal foursquare account, and download the app to your smartphone. Creating an account is easy. Foursquare just needs to know who you are and where you are. It also asks for a photo or avatar. This makes it easier for friends and businesses to recognize you. You'll want to do this. Now have fun. Check in to venues, leave tips (with photos if you'd like), add friends, and experience the full range of foursquare's offerings. This isn't an empty exercise. You cannot take a hands-off approach to foursquare and expect to develop creative ideas. All of the successful marketers in this book are active participants.

If you've never used foursquare, you might be surprised by what your customers are saying. Are they raving about

the fried chicken? Your servers should know about it. Do
they think your mojitos are too expensive for what they get?
Lower the price or make them stronger.

◆ **Claim your venue.** As a business owner, this is your first step
to establishing a digital dialogue with your customers. Search
for your venue on the foursquare website, and look for the
orange banner that says, "Do you manage this venue? Claim
here." Click it, and you will be directed to a page that walks
you through the process.

◆ **Leave tips.** Before you begin offering specials, you might
want to get your feet wet by leaving tips under your business account. Specials will be discussed in the next chapters.
For now, pay attention to what people are saying about your
business and what specials are being offered by competing
or neighboring venues. Based on your core mission, leaving tips and offering content might be the best way to use
foursquare.

CHAPTER 2

Connection Superstars

> *If your brand is a personal service, then you need to be personable with your customers.*
>
> —**MARIA AVGITIDIS,** Founder, Agape Match

How to unlock the Superstar badge
Check into 50 different venues.

ajor brands, local merchants, and nonprofits around the world are finding ways to connect with foursquare users by aligning their brand's unique value with the needs of the mobile user community. In this chapter, you will hear from two vastly different foursquare partners—a small business owner and a globally recognized organization. Both are foursquare superstars because they use the tool in ways that are completely aligned with their respective missions.

A Matchmaker Hooks Up with foursquare

MARIA AVGITIDIS
New York, New York

Maria Avgitidis is a fourth-generation matchmaker and founder of Agape Match, a matchmaking service that helps singles find love in the big city. She says the women in her Greek family all had a strong sixth sense about love and relationships (her grandmother once conducted Greek coffee readings to predict the romantic future of her clients). Maria still likes her coffee strong, but she uses a more modern tool to connect those looking for love—foursquare.

When Maria first moved to New York in 2009, she stumbled across foursquare and used it to learn more about her city. "For the first two months, I kept seeing it on my Facebook friends' pages or on Twitter posts. I thought, 'What is this and why are these people telling me where they are?'"[1] By accident she realized that when she checked in to places, word spread among her friends, and some would show up at the event, venue, or party.

Maria's epiphany moment occurred when she checked in to a local bar and posted a message that she was out with a group of ladies. "I'll never forget it. Twelve guys showed up—three of whom where following me on foursquare. They had brought friends. They said, 'We heard you had single ladies here.' That's when I realized that I could use foursquare to grow my brand."

Unlike many brands on foursquare that sell tangible products, food, or drinks, Maria's "product" is her reputation. She discovered a way to align foursquare with her brand and used the platform to build her reputation.

Setting Up Strangers for a Living

Avgitidis maintains a website (www.agapematch.com), a Twitter account, and a Facebook page. Foursquare does not replace those marketing channels. It enhances them. "I use my personality as a brand and to build a following. If you like me, you will follow me on foursquare to see where I check in. I tell you that there are single ladies there, and if you're single, you should come over."

Maria's business is all about meeting new people and connecting those people with their potential mates. New York is a city of eight million people and a place where women far outnumber men. Many women are looking for love but, as you would expect, they want to trust their matchmaker—whether it's a friend or a professional like Maria. Maria is personable and has an intriguing brand story. Foursquare simply extends her brand to a new category of clients who may never have discovered her service. She now has hundreds of followers on foursquare and well over 1,000 Facebook fans.

According to Maria, foursquare is responsible for one-third of her success. "Truth be told, had there not been social media tools, there is no way that I could have grown exponentially. Without Twitter, Facebook, and foursquare, it never would have happened."

39

Maria doesn't have a marketing budget, because *she doesn't need one*. Foursquare and social media have been that powerful for her. Foursquare is perfectly in sync with the service she offers and her clients' increasingly mobile lifestyles. "My brand is built on word of mouth and interacting with clients. That's enough to get me my next client." Maria's innovative approach to helping singles find love has helped her dating service rank her company, Agape Match, as one of the top dating services in New York City. She has also been featured on blogs, websites, and television news programs. It's no wonder this matchmaker has found love with foursquare.

A Badge of Honor

 AMERICAN RED CROSS
Washington, D.C.

Wendy Harman had been using foursquare since the service began. Part of the reason she joined as an early adopter is that her position as social media director requires that she learn about new social and mobile media tools. In addition there was a "fierce" competition to be the mayor of the location where she works. But although she was familiar with foursquare and had been a regular user, she didn't quite know how it would complement her organization's mission: to prevent and relieve pain and suffering.

Harman is the social media director for the American Red Cross, an organization founded in 1881 by visionary leader and innovator Clara Barton. The Red Cross provides many international services, including disaster relief and support for military families. Most of us see the Red Cross on television news when volunteers and employees spring into action when a natural disaster hits. But for four million people a year, the Red Cross has a more intimate connection—they are the ones that get a needle stuck in their arms to give blood. The Red Cross is the largest supplier of blood in the United States.

What can a blood supplier possibly have in common with a mobile social networking game? That's what Harman was asking herself when she met foursquare cofounder Dennis Crowley during a panel discussion. It didn't take long for a partnership to form.

The Red Cross is all about galvanizing communities—neighbors helping neighbors. It is not a government agency. It relies on donations of time, money, and blood to accomplish its mission and so requires a devoted group of evangelists to spread its message. "The people who use foursquare are the people we want to engage with the Red Cross,"[2] says Harman. As you know by now, foursquare users love to share their experiences with their social networks, most notably Facebook and Twitter. According to Harman, "It's a big deal to put a needle in your arm. If you are on Facebook, Twitter, or foursquare, you're going to talk about it."

So how did the American Red Cross make sure that people would talk about their experience with their friends? In exchange for giving blood, foursquare users would unlock a custom and exclusive blood donor badge—the American Red Cross badge. "It's a big deal to a lot of people," says Harman. "They are inclined to tell their friends about it. It's reinforcement that they are part of an amazing club of donors."

The campaign worked and continues to work, very well. "The reaction has been super positive," says Harman. She was

CHECKING IN

"Use foursquare personally first. It's like learning to drive a stick shift. You can't just read about it. You have to do it. We are in a period of extreme innovation on the social web. Get in there and figure it out. Once you use it yourself, you can think about some smart uses for your community, your nonprofit, or your business."

—**WENDY HARMAN,** Social Media Director, the American Red Cross right about sharing. Donors who link their foursquare account to Twitter automatically send their followers this message: "I just unlocked the 'American Red Cross' badge on @foursquare!" Users who unlock the badge are greeted with this message: "Congratulations! Your blood donation may have just helped to save a life."

Check in and Give the Gift of Life

In January 2011, a series of severe winter snowstorms shut down many parts of the eastern United States. The weather caused the cancellation of 14,000 blood and platelet donations through the American Red Cross, bringing supplies to the lowest January level in a decade. To put that in perspective, the American Red Cross typically needs 15,000 units of blood in one weekend just to keep up with demand on a regular day. The need for blood is constant. Every two seconds a patient in the United States needs a blood transfusion. A shortage of donations can cause some very serious problems for those who face life-threatening traumas.

42

The situation was so serious that the American Red Cross launched a national appeal for blood donors—something that it had not done since 2004. Fortunately the Red Cross foursquare campaign had been in place for two months prior to this emergency. Harman and her team announced the appeal across their existing social media platforms like the American Red Cross site, blog, Twitter, and Facebook. In each of the stories they reminded potential donors that they would be unlocking the Red Cross badge by donating and checking in on foursquare. "Everyone wants a badge, so it was very important," says Harman.

A longer-term benefit is widening the available pool of donors. Only about 2 percent of eligible blood donors actually donate blood, and the majority of those donors are older. The worst possible scenario would be for surgeries to be canceled or little blood available for disaster and trauma victims because donations are simply too low. The foursquare badge helps the American Red Cross align its brand with a new group of potential donors who enjoy doing good deeds and are more apt to share those good deeds with others, encouraging even more people to give a truly valuable gift—the gift of life.

🔓 UNLOCK THE POWER

- **See yourself as a brand.** Maria the date coach saw herself as a brand and acted as a brand to market and grow her business. You'll read about many global brands in this book, but as an individual you now have access to the same tools as those brands. And they're free!
- **Appeal to intrinsic motivators.** Many of the businesses and organizations that you will find on foursquare are offering tangible goods or services as a reward for a customer's loyalty. But don't forget that intrinsic motivators might work equally well, depending on the unique value of your business.

43

CHAPTER 3

Harness New Fans

"We want local merchants to create a new type of loyalty that goes beyond offers and discounts, but deepening and enhancing the connection between merchants and consumers."

—TRISTAN WALKER,
Vice President, Business Development, foursquare

During a recent visit to the East Coast I conducted a communications workshop for the sales team of a major media company. It was held at an off-site in Hoboken, New Jersey. As a proud Italian I was familiar with Hoboken as the home of one my boyhood heroes, Frank Sinatra, as well as the legendary Feast of San Gennaro. But other than its Italian and musical legacy, my surroundings were unfamiliar to me and I was eager to return to my hotel in Midtown Manhattan. Before heading to the train station to catch the 5:10 out of town, I opened my foursquare account. With that simple act my smartphone turned into a personalized tour guide, opening the gate to new and local discoveries. I got so wrapped up in exploring my local vicinity that I couldn't care less about missing the 5:10 back to New York City. Every neighborhood has a story to tell, and foursquare brings that story to life.

A New Discovery in Sinatra's Old Neighborhood

Once I had accessed foursquare in Hoboken, the app automatically used my smartphone's GPS to pinpoint my exact location. Foursquare also recognized that I was standing close to the corner of Hudson and 1st and pushed a special offer to my phone. I looked up and noticed that the special was brought to me by the restaurant across the street. It didn't turn out to be just any restaurant, but one of the most innovative restaurant concepts I've discovered in years. It was so intriguing, in fact, I took photos of the entrées and posted them to foursquare and to Twitter for all my friends and followers to see.

The restaurant that attracted me that day is called Energy Kitchen. The special itself caught my attention (free illy coffee for the mayor), but since I wasn't the mayor, it wasn't the only thing that encouraged me to visit the restaurant. What attracted me were the tips left by other fourquare users who clearly loved the food and the concept: Energy Kitchen offers wraps, burgers, and salads. No entrée is more than 500 calories, and everything is grilled, baked, or steamed. The restaurant takes the guesswork out of eating healthy. I thought it was a clever concept and had never seen anything quite like it before. I ordered the grilled salmon entrée with a side of broccoli and brown rice. Total calories: 445. And yes, it was deliciously prepared.

When I travel to New York City, it's hard for me to "be good" when it comes to keeping my calories in check. I like rich Italian food, great wine, pizza, and cheesecake, and as any visitor to New York will tell you, these items are available on every corner! If I could find someplace nearby with healthy and savory food, it would help me keep the pounds off before I went home to California. I was pleasantly surprised to learn that Energy Kitchen was a growing chain that had 10 establishments in Manhattan, and one was very close to where I was staying in Midtown. Thanks to its special offer and to the word-of-mouth endorsements on foursquare, Energy Kitchen had won a new fan—an evangelist, really.

"Why Aren't You on foursquare?"

When I returned to California—satisfied and healthier—I contacted Energy Kitchen's director of marketing. She told me that the restaurant had begun experimenting with foursquare just one month earlier. The restaurant's patrons were already checking in before foursquare caught the owners' attention. In fact the restaurant's existing customers were the ones who were having conversations about the menu and sharing those tips with their friends well before the brand itself recognized what was happening. "Why aren't you on foursquare?" Energy Kitchen customers would ask.

More than 1,500 customers had already checked in before foursquare was brought to the attention of Energy Kitchen's marketing department. This is a common story repeated by most of the businesses featured in this book. Foursquare's users are so enthusiastic about the service that they are the ones who typically are the first ones to bring it to the business owners' attention. Think about it. When is the last time you had a customer pitch you on a service or company in which they had no vested financial interest? It doesn't happen very often, if at all. Foursquare users are different, and that's why as a local merchant you need to introduce yourself to them, really get to know them, and engage them.

Once foursquare was brought to Energy Kitchen's attention, they began to get acquainted with it by simply monitoring the conversations that people were already having about their brand. They found that the conversations were different than those shared on Twitter or Facebook. Users were sharing real insider tips.

Energy Kitchen then took a three-step approach to developing a foursquare strategy to help attract new customers:

1. **Watch**. The marketing director downloaded the free foursquare app to her smartphone and started watching and learning about what other brands were doing and what customers were saying about those brands. She noticed that customers really enjoyed being recognized for their loyalty. Mayors would post their new status to Twitter and Facebook.

2. **Attract.** Energy Kitchen entered the foursquare world by offering a reward for the mayor at each of their locations. Since they were promoting specialized illy coffee drinks at the time, the restaurant decided to offer a free coffee for the mayor anytime he or she checked in during the month. No purchase was required. As you can imagine, the mayors felt very special, and it sparked competition among friends to

attain the status, attracting new customers and rewarding loyal patrons.

3. **Communicate.** Energy Kitchen spread the word about its special on its Twitter and Facebook pages. Using Twitter and Facebook to complement foursquare is a very common technique among merchants who are successfully unlocking the full power of the mobile app. Customers of Energy Kitchen are already evangelists for the brand. Combined with foursquare evangelists who are equally as passionate about the foursquare brand, Energy Kitchen found a winning formula. Foursquare users began telling their friends about Energy Kitchen's offer. Word spread quickly.

Energy Kitchen's experiment with foursquare, in one month alone, attracted more than 400 new customers, and the frequency of check-ins among existing foursquare users who patronize the restaurants grew exponentially. The results were impressive enough that Energy Kitchen continues to experiment with specials and rewards. One creative idea was to designate one day per month as Mayor Appreciation Day and to give each mayor on that day a free wrap, burger, or salad.

49

CHECKING IN

It's important that every customer-facing employee in your company knows about your foursquare campaign. At Energy Kitchen, the marketing director first explained the idea to senior staff and then sent a newsletter to all employees that included a mock-up of a phone with the special. Employees and cashiers were given step-by-step instructions, and the company reported no problems during the campaign. In fact, some of their employees reminded the mayors that they were entitled to free coffee!

Social media is not advertising according to the marketing director of Energy Kitchen. Instead, she likens it to taking the "pulse" of your customer on the street. It's a far different way to talk to your customers than you otherwise would do by running a traditional print ad or offering direct-mail coupons. The marketing director told me that by using traditional media only, Energy Kitchen could never have paid for the amount of value it received from using foursquare in their strategy.

A Crowdsourced Version of a Sales Force

Foursquare's users love specials, and they love being rewarded for their loyalty. When foursquare was looking for more ways to get more businesses on the platform, they simply tapped in to the best sales force they could find: their own users. Foursquare users are so eager for merchants to engage them and to reward them for their loyalty, they have become foursquare's sales evangelists. "Every company that I've worked at has a floor of people making cold calls. We don't,"[1] says foursquare cofounder Dennis Crowley in an exclusive interview for this book. "Merchants hear about specials and mayors—but not by us. Our users tell them about it. Our superusers are a crowdsourced version of a sales force."

Foursquare gives its superfans an innovative way to get involved in building the company. It's called the foursquare Ambassador Program. It's a simple idea. Passionate foursquare users who want to get more specials in their areas can fill out a form on the foursquare website to be chosen as ambassadors. If approved, users are sent a pack of ambassador cards (custom-printed with their names). They can hand out these cards to local businesses. The businesses attract new customers, and the ambassador gets to see more specials at their favorite places. The ambassadors are not getting paid. They are not working on commission. They are doing so because they are passionate about foursquare.

A 36,000 Percent Return on a $5 Investment

In January 2011, my wife and I decided to get away for a couple of days to the wine region of Paso Robles, California. Paso is growing in popularity because of its award-winning Rhone varietals, "big" zinfandels, and limestone soil that is ideal for growing flavorful grapes. There are now many more than 200 wineries in this small appellation between the San Francisco Bay area and four hours north of Los Angeles. With that many wineries, it's difficult to discover new places unless you read about it in *Wine Spectator* or hear about a particular winery through word of mouth. On this particular trip, I opened foursquare and was not surprised to find that no wineries offered foursquare specials, except for one: Opolo Vineyards.

Opolo is tucked about two miles from the main artery, Highway 4, in the rugged Santa Lucia Mountains. It's known for its "Mountain Zin," a 16.7 percent alcohol bomb that is sure to please the palette of those who enjoy the fruit-forward, high-alcohol zin style that has become the signature of California's zinfandel producers.

During this particular trek through wine country, we noticed that Opolo was the only winery offering a special—complimentary tasting for first-time check-ins (see Figure 3.1). Vanessa and I had just stopped at another winery down the road. We decided to visit Opolo because of its foursquare special. Now, saving $5 on the tasting fee didn't really matter to us, but the special made Opolo stand out among its competitors (places with specials are highlighted on the foursquare app). The special itself attracted new visitors—my wife and I. Since we are both active smartphone users, we fall into a desirable demographic of customers who are more likely to spend money.

We enjoyed the wines at Opolo so much that we signed up for its club membership ($120 per quarter). We were also told that Opolo had its own inn—a beautiful and secluded

FIGURE 3.1

Opolo Vineyards offers a special for first-time check-ins.

bed-and-breakfast that overlooked the vineyards. We stayed at Opolo on our next visit and decided that it was an undiscovered treasure—gorgeous rooms, magnificent view, wonderful service, and your own personal chef!

Let's do the math: wine purchased on day of check-in, $70; annual wine club membership, $500; room rate (two separate visits in one year), $1,200. Now think what had happened that day thanks to a foursquare special. Two people decided to take a road trip on a winding road surrounded by vineyards. They were attracted by a special and contributed nearly $1,800 to a small winery's bottom line in 2011. This happened because the winery had done something simple that its neighboring wineries had not bothered to do. Total cost to Opolo: $5 for the tasting, which they would have waived anyway because we signed up for the club membership. That's a 36,000 percent return on their money. Are you getting it? Foursquare helps you harness new customers for free.

I was surprised that foursquare had such a robust following in a remote wine country region in central California. Although few business establishments were offering specials in the area, we discovered many active foursquare users among the young staff working in the restaurants and wineries. One 23-year-old recent college graduate staffing a local winery told us that foursquare was "insanely popular" with her and her friends. She had hundreds of friends who followed each others' daily routines and shared tips and suggestions all day long. Your customers and staff are already using location-based services like foursquare. Shouldn't you be?

A foursquare Campaign Carrie Bradshaw Would Love

"Sex and the City" fans are well aware of character Carrie Bradshaw's love for shoes, especially shoes from the designer Jimmy Choo. Off screen, Jimmy Choo shoes are worn by Michelle Obama, Sandra Bullock, Madonna, and many other A-list celebrities and fashion icons. There really is a Jimmy behind the brand's name. Jimmy Choo is a Malaysian fashion designer based in London. Although he is best known for handmade women's shoes, the company that bears his name has become a global luxury shoe and accessories brand.

53

In May 2010, Jimmy Choo engaged London-based social media agency FreshNetworks to manage its social media campaign for a new collection. Jimmy Choo wanted to use social media to help launch a new line called "Trainers." Its objectives were to:

- attract new fans
- generate significant buzz about the new Trainers
- increase offline press coverage about the new shoes
- help position Jimmy Choo as a creative innovator in the space of social media
- increase positive sentiment about the Jimmy Choo brand
- increase sales

Based on these objectives, FreshNetworks, which managed Jimmy Choo's Twitter and Facebook presence, decided to add foursquare to the mix.

The new shoe line, Trainers, are designed for women who want to take a break from their high heels without compromising on style. The highly stylized shoes are made of suede and exotic snakeskin. They come in low- and high-tops and have tricked-out gold eyelets.

Since most Jimmy Choo shoes are purchased in brick-and-mortar stores, FreshNetworks recognized that they would need to engage customers online and attract them to stores offline. Foursquare's mission is to help people explore their city—to bridge the virtual with the physical—and so was perfectly aligned with Jimmy Choo's social media strategy. The FreshNetworks idea was creative and simple. Jimmy Choo would use foursquare to create a treasure hunt around London. Carrie Bradshaw would have loved it so much that she would have flown to London to participate. It worked very, very well.

FreshNetworks set up profiles on foursquare under the name of CatchAChoo to represent the new Trainers. A member of the FreshNetworks team would check in under the profile at fashionable hangouts in the city. The team member would then send real-time updates about his or her whereabouts on foursquare, Facebook, and Twitter. The Jimmy Choo Trainers checked in to hip places around town—from the Saatchi Gallery to the Shoreditch House. Whoever reached the venue in time to CatchAChoo would win a pair of Trainers in their size (the shoes start at 300 British pounds, the equivalent of about 480 U.S. dollars). Jimmy Choo advertised the Trainer hunt on its Twitter, Facebook, and foursquare pages in addition to its commerce website (see Figure 3.2).

According to FreshNetworks' marketing manager, Jo Stratmann, "The hunt lasted for almost three weeks until the Trainers were finally 'caught' by someone."[2] The person walked into a venue and discovered a Jimmy Choo team member holding a bag full of Trainers. Since only one person successfully caught the Choo, Jimmy Choo hosted an in-store event for the rest of the CatchAChoo followers to further deepen the bond they had formed with the brand.

FIGURE 3.2

Jimmy Choo advertises its foursquare Trainer hunt campaign.

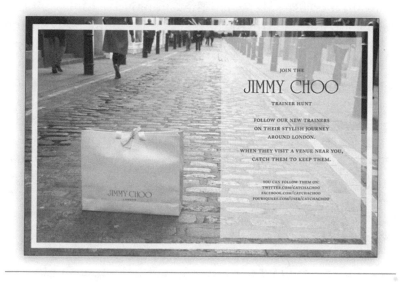

The campaign was an enormous success. But you might be asking, how can the campaign be considered a success if only one person received a free pair of shoes? In those three weeks, 4,000 people participated in the Jimmy Choo Trainer hunt on foursquare (about 1 in 17 of all London foursquare users at the time). This metric is astonishing. One brand encouraged 4,000 people to chase a shoe around London, and most of them shared their treasure hunt with other friends on their social networks. Details about the competition were viewed by more than 280,000 on Facebook and had garnered more than 4,000 mentions on Twitter. Other results included the following:

- 250 blogs covered the Jimmy Choo Trainer hunt. It was the most viewed story on *PR Week* the day the story was published.
- The Trainer hunt was covered offline by *Reuters*, *The Evening Standard*, and *Vogue*, among other magazines.
- Positive mentions about the Jimmy Choo brand increased by almost 40 percent as a result of the campaign.

The foursquare campaign has clearly satisfied most of Jimmy Choo's original objectives, but what about the last one—to increase sales? Had the campaign actually enticed people to drop $400 on the new shoes? Yes, it had. According to Stratmann, "Daily Trainer sales in-store went up 33 percent during the three weeks of the Jimmy Choo Trainer hunt campaign." Stratmann also found evidence that the campaign had worked to attract new fans to the Jimmy Choo brand. Jimmy Choo doesn't need foursquare to put it on the map. It's already there. But it needs to stay relevant, contemporary, and competitive. Mobile marketing helps the brand do just that.

Free Wings with a Side of Eye Candy

Local merchants who are using mobile marketing to successfully attract new customers are those who are being aggressive with their foursquare specials. Their specials are bold and buzzworthy. They're not waiting for their competitors to get there first. They are paving the way for others to follow. When it comes to social media, they're all in.

A Hooters regional manager in Kansas City, Missouri, began offering 10 free wings for every check-in. Not for the first check-in or the fifth check-in—but *every* check-in.

Buffalo and chicken wings are Hooters' signature dish. Well, the chain's signature food item. As its name would suggest, diners visit Hooters for a lot more than wings. This particular manager created the offer and applied it to all his restaurants in the region. By getting ahead of the curve and offering aggressive specials, he told me that the restaurants are drawing patrons who have not dined at Hooters for a while. The Hooters manager also started a promotion called foursquare Friday and offered 16 percent off the total bill for any diner who checked in and unlocked the special. Why 16 percent and not 15? The manager liked 16 because it's "4 squared."

The campaigns worked. Each restaurant began report-
ing that patrons who unlocked the wings special were apt
to return. Yes, they were returning for free wings and the
other "features" Hooters is famous for; but they returned,
and when they did, they ordered a lot more than the free
wings.

A Rainy Day Special That Brightened Sales

Many local merchants are learning that foursquare can attract
customers during slow periods. Just as bars and taverns
provide discounts during happy hours to attract a crowd, foursquare merchants are finding that offering specials increases
use in times of excess capacity—in other words, they bring
feet in the door when those feet are needed the most.

If you own a chain of bicycle stores like Mike's Bikes in
northern California, rain is not your friend. Very few people
walk into a bike shop when it's wet outside. But there are
still die-hards who ride. Managers at Mike's Bikes noticed an
interesting trend at their Sausalito store, across the Golden
Gate Bridge from San Francisco. Riders at that location meet
up in the parking lot before their treks, especially on weekends. But on rainy days they did not go into the store. That
is, until Mike's Bikes launched a foursquare special that took
just a few minutes to set up: Rainy day special! Bring your
helmet into Mike's Bikes today and get 20 percent off all bike
accessories.

It worked. Slowly at first, but over several rainy weekends,
more and more riders would redeem the special. They also
told their friends about it in the parking lot. Those riders who
were not on foursquare joined the service to take advantage of
the offer.

Because foursquare makes it easy to update specials,
Mike's Bikes will often change its specials to keep it fresh,
attract new customers, and offer incentives to customers who

CHECKING IN

Create specials that stand out for being bold or unique. Restaurant Max in Minneapolis, Minnesota, offered a creative special: check in on the week of your birthday and get a free bottle of wine worth your age. It seems age does count in wine and on foursquare.

had unlocked an earlier special. Riders will often find that the specials change from one weekend to the next based on the season, the weather, or due to a particular weekend event in the neighborhood. One rainy day special announced: Bring your helmet into Mike's Bikes and win a Mike's Bikes patch kit.

On typical, nonrainy days, foursquare users might find a playful special such as: 20 percent off clothing or components when you come in kitted up with a helmet (we'll even hang on to your purchases until after you ride) or 20 percent off bike accessories when you show this special at checkout. During the summer, Mike's Bikes encourages repeat visits with specials such as: Free Mike's Bikes water bottle on your fifth check-in! Mike's Bikes has discovered a powerful new tool to share its story. Best of all, it's free. It takes five minutes to update a special, and it's working.

Tristan Walker, foursquare's vice president of business development, says sole proprietors and local merchants (think Joe's Coffee, Mary's Flowers, or other small businesses) are joining foursquare by the tens of thousands because they recognize the power of adding specials to attract new customers. "When you talk to these merchants you find out that they care about two things—retention and acquisition,"[3] says Walker. "They are asking themselves, how do I get customers to walk in and how do I get customers to return. Foursquare can help you with both."

An Optometrist with an Eye for foursquare

Dr. Nate Bonilla-Warford is well known in the Tampa community as the owner of Bright Eyes, a family eye-care office that specializes in infants, children's vision, and vision therapy. His patients can schedule eye exams or buy glasses and contact lenses, and this being a doctor's office, they can find plaques as well. Dr. Nate received a Doctorate of Optometry and displays his plaque proudly. But Dr. Nate is also proud of another honor that he displays prominently on the wall of his office—the founder of foursquare Day.

April 16 of 2010 marked the first official foursquare Day around the world. Thousands of loyal foursquare users hosted parties and events while local merchants offered extra-special specials to entice customers. Dr. Nate didn't just participate; he started it. Foursquare Day was first conceived, planned, and promoted in his Tampa office. From behind his computer, Dr. Nate unknowingly ignited a worldwide movement that reflects the true power of foursquare.

Dr. Nate has always been a fan of social media. His office maintains active Facebook and Twitter pages. He was a fan of foursquare even before he could use it himself. Dr. Nate's friends in New York introduced him to foursquare, and the day after foursquare became available in Tampa, he blogged about it. Dr. Nate held informal social media workshops for local business owners, and he wanted to teach them about foursquare.

On March 12, 2010, Dr. Nate had an idea. Why not designate April 16th as foursquare Day? Since April is the fourth month of the year, and the number 16 is 4 squared, he thought it might be a fun way to introduce his staff and others in the community to the service. He floated the idea on Twitter and his blog. The idea began to attract supporters, and on March 22nd, a Facebook page had been created for the event. On March 26th, foursquare embraced it and posted an announcement to Twitter.

Word of the event began to spread, slowly at first and then more quickly than Dr. Nate could keep up. Users took to Twitter, Facebook, and blogs to share their excitement and to plan parties. The event was soon billed as the "first global social media holiday." Parties and celebrations were hosted in 100 major cities, including Seoul, Budapest, Kuala Lumpur, Sydney, and of course, Tampa. Users could either join the foursquare Day Fan Page on Facebook or promote their participation on Twitter by using the hashtag #4sqday.

Looking back on the event, Dr. Nate is still stunned that all of this happened when foursquare had 500,000 users. By the next foursquare Day in 2011, the platform had grown to about eight million users, and events were held on all corners of the planet. As previously mentioned, New York City Mayor Michael Bloomberg even proclaimed the date foursquare Day in the city. Dr. Nate didn't know it at the time he first conceived of foursquare Day, but he had launched a global movement. This Tampa eye doctor had turned into a social-media hero.

Social media observers who wrote about the event said it reflects the power of foursquare and other social media tools to give the average person tremendous reach, influence, and power. Nobody was more surprised than Dr. Nate. Although he had been blogging for years, he never fully appreciated the almost limitless power of social media until this idea went viral. He simply wanted to plan a simple foursquare celebration in his Tampa office. "The tools of social media have a powerful long reach. They allow us to explore other cultures, ideas, and concepts. But they also allow communities to connect from within."[4]

I included the story of Dr. Nate in this chapter about attracting new customers because as a merchant, brand, or retailer who offers a foursquare special, these are the type of evangelists you are going to attract and these are the type of customers you would *want* to attract.

How many businesses have customers who would create a special day in their honor? How many companies have users who voluntarily stamp temporary tattoos on themselves to celebrate their membership? Don't believe me? Visit Google images and search for foursquare tattoos (these tattoos are ubiquitous at conferences like South by Southwest where foursquare was first launched). The people who cover their arms or torsos with tattoos of foursquare badges are not fair-weather customers. They are fanatical, loyal, and eager to share their excitement—about foursquare and for merchants like you who engage them.

Welcome to the Merchant Platform

Setting up a special on foursquare is easy, free, and fun. It all begins with foursquare's Merchant Platform, which allows a mom-and-pop to compete with a national chain to attract new customers and reward their most loyal ones. You can create up to seven different specials for every type of customer—from newbies to mayors (foursquare mayorships are awarded to customers with the most days checked in to your venue over the last 60 days. Only users who have uploaded photo profiles are eligible, which means the mayor's photo will always be available to you as a merchant on your venue page). The Merchant Platform also gives you access to venue stats—a dashboard—rich with details about your customers (more on dashboard analytics later). For now, keep in mind that specials—especially "aggressive" ones—will attract new customers to your venue.

There are three ways for foursquare users to discover your special:

1. When users are looking at the nearby places on the app, venues that have active specials are highlighted.
2. When a user checks in to a business near you—but not your place—he or she will see that there is a "special nearby." By clicking the banner, that user will be taken to your special.
3. When a user checks in to your business, he or she will see your special.

The Day My Wife Became a foursquare Fan

I remember exactly where I was standing when my wife, Vanessa, "got" the idea behind foursquare and became a fan. We were shopping at our local mall, and I had just opened foursquare to check in. (This particular mall, by the way, offers a designated parking spot for the foursquare mayor. If you're the mayor of a mall, however, you might want to reconsider your spending habits!) Upon checking in, I noticed a special nearby. I clicked the orange banner and up popped a special for a store called Express. I had never been there nor had my wife, although we had passed it countless times. In fact my wife told me that she never shopped at Express. She's a Nordstrom's kind of girl. The special was sufficiently enticing to attract us: Get $25 off a $75 purchase or $50 off $150.

"Wait a minute. We can save $25 or $50 just by showing them your phone?" my wife asked incredulously.

"Well, we have to check in first to unlock it," I explained.

"Oh, and how long will that take?" my wife asked.

"About two seconds. I just have to tap the screen."

Two seconds (and 30 minutes) later we were showing my phone to the cashier and paying for $175 worth of merchandise. Express had attracted two new customers, and foursquare had attracted a new evangelist. My wife has since convinced dozens of friends and local merchants to join foursquare. By offering a foursquare special, Express had won over a loyal, repeat customer—not simply a customer who entered the store one time only to redeem a coupon. You see, my wife returned the next week for a necklace that she had spotted on her first visit. Since it did not cost $75, she could not unlock the special. It didn't matter. She returned to the store and will probably return again, special or no special. I just hope she doesn't earn the designated mayor's parking space, or I'll have to hide my wallet!

I read a statistic that 19 percent of kids ages two to nine can operate a smartphone app, yet only 9 percent of those kids can tie their shoes. It won't take long for your customers to learn about foursquare and other mobile marketing tools. And if they don't know about it, you can teach them. You might live or do business in a community that has fewer foursquare users than you find in a large city, and in that case, it might take more time to create some buzz. But it will happen, especially as more of your customers become comfortable with checking in.

When I started writing this book, I was the only one who checked in to the farmers' market in my small town about 50 miles east of San Francisco. I often write on Saturday mornings, and the market is outside my office building in downtown Pleasanton. A few weeks into my writing I noticed that three others had checked in. Two weeks later, six had checked in, and one month later, one dozen people had checked in on foursquare. I told the owner of a great restaurant near the market that he should join foursquare and create a special for farmers' market Saturdays. That's the way it builds—through word of mouth online and offline.

63

UNLOCK THE POWER

- **Create a fabulous special.** Once you claim your venue and foursquare has verified your business, use the Merchant Platform to create a special offer. Be aggressive to generate buzz among foursquare users and your local community. Mobile social media rewards bold initiatives.
- **Train your staff.** Have you ever dined at a restaurant where the waitstaff knew very little about the menu or that night's specials? It happens quite often, doesn't it? Well it happens on foursquare, too. I walked into a toy store and asked about a foursquare special the chain was promoting. I even showed the cashier the special on my smartphone. She had no clue. This happens from time to time as some businesses create

social media programs just because they don't want to be "left out." Unfortunately they launch the campaign before having a strategy in place or adequately training their staff. Align your campaign with your brand, offer a meaningful special, and make sure everyone knows about the special and how to apply the discount in the system.

◆ **Change the Specials . . . Often.** One tavern owner I spoke to changes his specials almost every week—a Monday special is different than a Friday special. Different times of the week attract different crowds, and his specials are uniquely customized to the audience. Changing the specials frequently keeps your brand fresh, creates loyalty, and generates repeat visits.

CHAPTER 4

Newbie Ringleaders

> " *How do you get someone to come into your restaurant instead of another? We now have a way of saying, come to us instead.* "
>
> —**NICOLE COCHRAN,** Marketing Director, Chili's Grill & Bar

How to unlock the Newbie badge
All foursquare users receive this badge upon checking in for the first time.

oursquare and other mobile social networking tools have huge implications for small and large businesses alike, including nonprofits. Innovative organizations are using foursquare to attract customers or reach new supporters. Chili's is a large U.S.-based chain restaurant that is standing out from its competitors by offering a surprisingly simple enticement. Earthjustice is a San Francisco Bay area nonprofit that does not have a need to attract customers to a physical location but used a physical location to attract new donors. Both stories show the power of foursquare to attract new customers or supporters in ways that were never possible until now.

Spicing Up Chips and Salsa

CHILI'S GRILL & BAR
Dallas, Texas

Chili's has been spicing up the casual dining scene since 1975 when it started as a burger joint in Dallas, Texas. Today Chili's shares its classic American Southwest recipes with diners at 1,500 locations around the world. Chili's is popular because the food is tasty, the bar menu is extensive, and it has something for everyone: Big Mouth burgers, savory ribs, fajitas, tacos, chicken, seafood, steaks, soups, salads, and popular deserts like molten chocolate cake and brownie sundaes.

It's not a challenge for Chili's to keep its customers satisfied. The food and service keep diners coming back. Chili's does have a more difficult challenge attracting customers who are deciding where to dine when they see a sea of casual dining spots in the same area: Chili's, Applebee's, TGI Friday's, Ruby Tuesday. Most people would be hard-pressed to tell the difference between these chains. They are very different, but most diners don't know it. Marketing experts in the casual dining category call it "the sea of sameness." The holy grail for such marketers is to stand out in this sea.

"We wanted to reach people at the point of their decision,"[1] says Nicole Cochran, Chili's marketing director. "With foursquare we now have a way to say, 'come to us instead of to a competitor. We're going to reward you for that decision.' That's a very appealing proposition." Cochran and her marketing team had been looking for ways to leverage mobile marketing technology. Since Chili's also has physical store locations, Cochran decided that a location-based service was a great idea. Chili's customers were already using foursquare, even before being rewarded for their loyalty (more than 800 Chili's locations had mayors).

Cochran used one of Chili's signature items as the hook to attract diners at this point of decision—chips and salsa. Diners love this appetizer. They post pictures online and try to replicate the recipe. Unlike Mexican restaurants that offer chips and salsa for free, Chili's charges $3 for the dish—unless you're on foursquare.

Chili's became the first national dining chain to offer guests a free menu item with every foursquare check-in. Here's how it works. Let's say a hungry driver pulls off the highway and sees a string of casual dining chains lining the street. He wants to sit down for a good meal and get back on the road within an hour, but he's having trouble deciding. If he opens foursquare and is near the vicinity of a participating Chili's, he will see the orange special banner appear in the list of places. It reads,

Welcome to Chili's Grill & Bar. Check in @ Chili's & get free Chips & Salsa on every check-in! Simply show your server the screen after checking-in!

The foursquare user simply has to check in to Chili's to unlock the special. He shows the server his phone with the special and gets his free appetizer. And of course, our hungry driver doesn't just eat his chips and leave. He buys higher-ticket items and leaves on a full stomach. Creating the special was free for Chili's. Although the restaurant gave away a $3 item, it more than made up for it after the diner's total bill, and it attracted a guest it might have lost to a competitor. Chili's stood out in the sea of sameness.

Cochran continues to experiment with foursquare specials because she sees results. It's also free. "There isn't much risk, because we make money on the deal, and it's clearly appealing, because we see an increasing number of check-ins every week." When Chili's first launched the special, it was recording more than 6,500 check-ins per week. The most telling statistic, however, is when Chili's compares the foursquare special to traditional coupons that Chili's sends via e-mail. "We can prove that coupons are incremental to our business," says Cochran. "And with foursquare, we're seeing double the redemption rate of our e-mail coupons."

Cochran didn't realize it at the time, but she did something so new and innovative with foursquare that Chili's received a ton of free press and blog mentions. The innovation? Giving something free to everyone who checked in. Cochran wasn't

CHECKING IN

"Make it easy for your servers to redeem the coupon. We have 80,000 employees, so we had to make it easy for everyone to understand the offer. We added eight words to the redemption screen: 'Chili's servers, use coupon code #23 to redeem.' We haven't heard of any problems."

—**NICOLE COCHRAN,** Marketing Director, Chili's Grill & Bar trying to be innovative. She did it out of necessity. Since four-square was still in its infancy when Chili's launched the promotion, she thought it would simply be too complicated to execute multitiered specials across hundreds of locations and 80,000 employees. Her solution to give something to everyone went viral. Diners who unlock the special are so excited about it they tend to share their enthusiasm with friends on Twitter and Facebook, generating free buzz and publicity for Chili's. The next time you get lost in the sea of sameness, check out Chili's check-in special to find your way out.

Checking In to Save a Critter from Checking Out

 EARTHJUSTICE
Oakland, California

69

Foursquare proved to be a grand slam for a tiny critter the size of a tennis ball. The pika, a mammal that is related to rabbits, lives in high elevations in the mountains of the American West and is susceptible to spikes in temperature. The small animal can die in less than an hour when the heat rises higher than 75 degrees Fahrenheit. Animal rights activists argue that global warming and rising temperatures are threatening pikas and other endangered species.

Earthjustice, a nonprofit public interest law firm, created an innovative foursquare campaign to tell the pika's story to thousands of people who could help save the species. An anonymous supporter agreed to donate up to $50,000 to support the cause. The catch—the donor wanted to raise awareness for the issue as well as other environmental problems. He wasn't interested in simply cutting a check. It would be up to Earthjustice to engage individuals. Earthjustice wanted its campaign to be unique and to appeal to the San Francisco Bay area audience, many of whom were environmentally conscious and tech savvy. Foursquare offered the right fit.

Earthjustice had just been granted billboard space at Bay Area Rapid Transit (BART) subway stations in the Bay Area. "The billboards, along with the willing donor, gave us the perfect storm of the right medium, the right campaign at the right time,"[2] says Earthjustice marketing manager Ray Wan. "We didn't want to do just another traditional ad. We wanted to engage people on environmental issues, but do it in a way that's fun, cutting-edge, and ultimately productive. Foursquare was the perfect fit for us because people are already using their smartphones as they're standing around waiting for the trains."

Posters were placed throughout the subway stations. Figure 4.1 shows that one ad read: "What does it take to help save

FIGURE 4.1

Earthjustice placed posters like this one in subway stations to urge people to check in to their ad on foursquare.

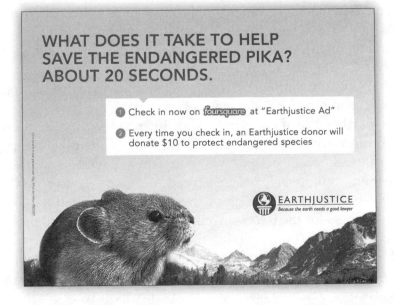

the endangered pika? About 20 seconds." The billboard urged individuals to check in on foursquare at the Earthjustice ad. It explained that for every check-in, a donor would contribute $10 to protect endangered species. A similar billboard read: "Don't just stand there. Stand there and help keep Tahoe's water clean." Every check-in would be matched with a $10 donation to help protect the water quality in Lake Tahoe, Nevada, the largest alpine lake in North America.

The billboards stayed up for six weeks. Thousands of people saw the posters, and 6,000 of them took the extra step to check in, easily earning the $50,000 contribution the donor had guaranteed. The campaign proves that a business or nonprofit need not have a physical location like a restaurant or bar to take advantage of these new mobile social media tools. Earthjustice took a creative approach to an old problem— raising money for its causes. The nonprofit tapped into a city that is passionate about the environment, technology, and smartphones.

Foursquare helped Earthjustice accomplish four things. First, it raised $50,000 to help the firm fund its environmental causes, including the pika and Tahoe campaigns.

Second, it attracted an entirely new generation of activists. According to Wan, prior to the foursquare campaign, Earthjustice donors had been made up largely of foundations, longtime sponsors, or older individuals who responded

CHECKING IN

"Although we couldn't give the mayor of the billboards a badge or a 'discount,' we could make them feel good about doing a good deed. We sent mayors a special thank-you e-mail and provided press links about the campaign. Think creatively about rewarding your foursquare supporters."

—**RAY WAN,** Earthjustice Director of Marketing

to mail-in campaigns. The foursquare campaign reached an entirely new audience of younger, tech-savvy, environmentally aware people in the Bay Area. A 27-year-old said he checked in to the ads at various BART stations as he commuted between home, college, and work. He said he passed subway billboards ever day, mostly for banks. The Earthjustice ads caught his attention and offered him a chance to protect an endangered animal by simply clicking a check-in tab on his smartphone.

Third, since most foursquare users automatically link their foursquare check-ins to their Facebook and Twitter accounts, the nonprofit reached an even larger audience than those who were physically standing in front of the billboards with their smartphones.

And fourth, since the campaign was one of the first to let people check in at a billboard, it generated free publicity for the nonprofit, including a story in the *New York Times*. CNN called as well to learn more about how Earthjustice created and ran the program.

The Earthjustice campaign resulted in numerous inquiries from nonprofits and other organizations that wanted to experiment with the platform to engage their existing supporters and to communicate their brand stories to an entirely new audience. The campaign is an example of a group of dedicated individuals tapping social networking and location-based services to make a difference in the world.

If you ever visit Lake Tahoe, one of the most beautiful places on Earth, you might take a slightly different look at the sparkling, emerald-blue water that covers the lake's 22 miles. And while you might never see a pika on your trip to the Sierra Nevada, it, too, might owe its survival to foursquare and a group of dedicated individuals who took an innovative approach to help solve some tough problems.

UNLOCK THE POWER

- **Train your staff.** This point cannot be stressed enough. Make sure everyone on your staff (including the person who answers the phone) knows about your mobile marketing initiatives and can explain it to your customers.
- **Give something to everyone.** Foursquare's merchant platform allows you to create multiple specials at the same time. It's great to attract new customers, but don't forget about your repeat customers either.

CHAPTER 5

Engage Your Followers

> **Engagement is our business objective. We're building a real relationship in a virtual space.**
>
> —CHRISTINA SPONSELLI,
> Social Media Director, University of California, Berkeley

The Green Bay Packers beat the Pittsburgh Steelers in Super Bowl XLV by a score of 31 to 25. Packers quarterback Aaron Rodgers threw for 303 yards and three touchdowns while Pittsburgh committed three costly turnovers. The price of a 30-second television spot was $3 million. With a U.S. audience of 111 million, it became the most-watched Super Bowl in television history. Those stats mattered to football fans, television executives, and advertisers. The social media community was abuzz over another key data point: 200,000. That's the number of foursquare users who checked in to "Super Bowl Sunday" from parties around the world and "shouted" the name of their favorite team (a shout-out is just what it sounds like—sending a short message to your friends).

By checking in and shouting their team's name, foursquare users earned a customized badge with the logo of the Packers or the Steelers. The badge came with a coupon discount of 20 percent that users could redeem at the NFL's online store, www.nflshop.com.

By kickoff about 40,000 people had checked in to Super Bowl Sunday. Thirty minutes later it had surpassed 60,000, and two hours later the number of check-ins had climbed to higher than 100,000, as foursquare users were unlocking the badge and sharing the information on Twitter and Facebook. In four hours, Super Bowl Sunday became foursquare's most checked-in venue ever. Many of the check-ins did occur at Cowboys Stadium in Arlington, Texas, where the game was played, but many users checked in from all parts of the world. Fans checked in from all 50 states, 125 countries, and the Vatican. Yes, 13 people checked in from the Vatican, proving that the Super Bowl was indeed The Big Game.

It was the first time that foursquare experimented with such "promoted venues" where people could check in to a place even though they were not at the location. The NFL entered the partnership with foursquare because it recognized that foursquare is more than a tool to entice customers to walk through the door. It's a powerful new way for brands, merchants, and other businesses to engage their supporters or customer base on a far deeper level than traditional advertising.

When Packers quarterback Aaron Rodgers was named the game's most valuable player, the cheers could be heard 1,700 miles away in the college town of Berkeley, California. Rodgers attended the University of California, Berkeley, where he played football and set several records for the Golden Bears. Coincidentally, Cal Berkeley is one of the most active foursquare college communities in the nation and a model for how foursquare can be used as a tool of engagement.

How Cal Berkeley Builds Real Relationships in a Virtual Space

UC Berkeley or "Cal" is the oldest of the 10 major campuses in the University of California system. It's considered one of America's great public institutions of higher learning. Berkeley is also recognized as the birthplace of the Free Speech Movement, with campus protests in the mid-1960s that inspired anti–Vietnam War protests across the country. Today the Berkeley campus bears little resemblance to the tumultuous hotbed of activism that it was in the 1960s.

Berkeley is admired for the quality of instruction (65 Nobel laureates have been university faculty, alumni, or researchers), difficult admissions requirements (the law school admits 270 students from more than 7,000 applicants), and its Pac 10 football and basketball teams. But stroll around the sprawling 1,200-acre campus with foursquare and history comes alive. A visitor within a few hundred yards of the Free Speech Movement Café is prompted to stop in, grab a bite, and learn

FIGURE 5.1

Cal Berkeley uses foursquare to encourage users to stop in at the Free Speech Movement Café.

more about the movement that gave the café its name (see Figures 5.1 and 5.2). Attend a Cal Bears football game at Memorial Stadium, and you'll learn that the stadium was built in 1923 and drew 73,000 for the big game with Stanford (Cal won). Curious about the blue and gold color of the uniforms? When you buy a ticket at the Cal ticket office, you might learn that Cal's founders were mostly Yale men who had come west. The gold represents the Golden State of California and the blue is Yale blue. Need a break during your tour? No problem. Drop in to the recreational sports facility, and get a discount on a massage (25 minutes for $25). The special was offered for a limited time only and could be unlocked only by a visitor with a foursquare account who showed his or her smartphone at the front desk.

Forty-five years after launching the Free Speech Movement, Berkeley is acting as a flash point for the mobile social movement. "Foursquare is a natural fit for us given the demographic of its users and our students,"[1] according to Berkeley's social media director, Christina Sponselli, who took me on a tour of the campus with foursquare in hand. "Younger people are using it. When they are new to the campus and living away from home, they build new social connections and friendships. They are also learning to navigate a large campus that is spread out geographically. Foursquare is perfectly suited

78

FIGURE 5.2

Outside the Free Speech Movement Café.

to helping them learn more about the campus and to connect socially."

"What are you trying to achieve?" I asked.

"Engagement," answered Sponselli. "Engagement is our business objective. Developing relationships and creating an experience for students, alumni, and friends like people who follow Cal football or donors who visit the campus. We're building a real relationship in a virtual space."

"How much is a relationship worth to a university like Berkeley?" I asked Sponselli.

CHECKING IN

Learn about foursquare and how your customers are using it by being actively engaged yourself. Don't just establish a venue, create a tip, or offer a special, and then forget about it. Sponselli frequently walks around campus, checks in through her individual account, reviews specials, and reads tips.

"A lot. These are our customers, and you want to take care of your customers. These are students attending our university, parents sending their kids here, or donors contributing their money to our institution. With foursquare, we offer ways to save money, learn more about the university, connect them with other people, and also give them bragging rights because they can unlock the 'Smells Like School Spirit' badge by visiting certain venues on campus. These are our ambassadors. And the people who support you are the best advertisers a university can have."

Sponselli makes a strong case for engaging your most ardent supporters. They are, after all, the best advertisers a company can have.

Reaching a Built-In Audience

College campuses and communities are finding a ready audience among their students who are constantly on their smartphones. They may forget their books, but they rarely forget their phones. Universities from Syracuse to Stanford are engaging their students and donors in a very similar way as Berkeley.

When I visited the Stanford campus to speak to MBA students at the Graduate School of Business, I learned a lot about the university thanks to foursquare and Stanford, which provides information on its own venue page. The content was intriguing, interesting, and fun. For example, the Quad is the center of campus. I knew that, but I had never heard of the Full Moon on the Quad: "Don't know what it is? Ask a student." So I did. It turns out the Full Moon is a mid-fall tradition where Stanford students kiss each other in the moonlight starting at midnight. I missed out on that tradition at my college.

Foursquare also taught me that the 14th floor of Hoover Tower provides the best views of the campus. I also learned that the basement of Jordan Hall was the scene for the notorious 1971 Stanford prison experiment—a psychological simulation of imprisonment that became so real ("guards" turned abusive) that the experiment was shut down early. Interesting stuff. In addition to the official Stanford-created content, students left many other tips on the best places to eat, study, and of course, party.

Since foursquare acts as a mobile friend-finder, it really is perfectly tailored for the campus environment. Picture a student getting out of class on a Friday afternoon, glancing at foursquare, and finding 10 friends eating at the dining hall or a nearby restaurant. Two of the students' friends are in the gym, another eight are at the pavilion to watch the volleyball game, while another shouted the location for a fraternity party that night. It's no wonder that foursquare is increasingly popular at universities. Schools like Cal, Stanford, Syracuse, Texas Tech, and many others are taking advantage of foursquare's mobile community and adding content, tips, specials, and customized badges to enhance the experience and engage their students. Any business establishment on or near a college campus should be paying attention to the mobile social networking trend.

The key for college marketing professionals is to get all departments involved: admissions, athletics, dining services, and so on. Once several departments are in the mix, the community becomes much more vibrant. The dining hall might offer custom specials, while the athletic teams and on-campus services offer their own. You might see the athletics department offer free apparel, water bottles, or other enticements like priority seating to people who check in to sporting events.

Colleges are just one example of how innovative organizations are leveraging location-based service (LBS) to engage their communities. The people who they are trying to engage might already be using the facilities, but organizations or companies will use foursquare to establish an even deeper, more meaningful relationship with those users.

Driving Is So 2008

Would riding public transit be more fun if you competed with other riders for points, badges, and bragging rights for being a "transit warrior?" Would you be more enticed to explore your neighborhood if you had insider tips from locals? BART—Bay Area Rapid Transit—became the first public transit agency to partner with foursquare. The goal is to encourage people to leave their cars at home and to use public transportation instead. BART recognized that by tapping into foursquare's game mechanics, it could engage riders once they reached the station.

BART started its promotion by giving away free $25 train tickets to three winners randomly drawn from all foursquare users who checked in to BART stations. It also offered a special BART-themed badge called the Train Spotter badge for frequent riders who checked in 10 times. In addition, BART offered exclusive tips and ideas for riders who wanted to learn about interesting and fun things to do near BART stations.

Most Popular BART Tips
- **Rockridge BART Station:** Walk to Zachary's Pizza (5801 College Ave.). Crazy delicious deep-dish pizza; the spinach and mushroom and the Mediterranean, with artichokes and feta, are veggie faves.
- **Embarcadero BART Station:** Walk to Ferry Building Marketplace. Foodie heaven with gourmet shops for

everything from mushrooms to chocolate, oysters to olive oils. Plus a farmers' market on Tuesdays and Saturdays.
* **16th St. Mission BART:** It's worth the walk just a few blocks over on Valencia to try Four Barrel Coffee. Great java *and* tunes on vinyl—actual LPs on an old-school record-playing machine.

What's interesting about the last one, Four Barrel Coffee, is that the coffee shop itself is not actively engaging its customers on foursquare. Yet at the time of this writing, nearly 3,000 people had checked in more than 9,000 times. There's no way to know how many of those people discovered the venue from the BART tip, but it shows, once again, that customers are checking in to places already, and the owners or proprietors either don't know about it or they're not taking advantage of the free opportunity to establish a deeper connection with these loyal customers.

The program works to engage BART's riders, and the public transit agency can prove it. BART surveyed about 450 riders and found that 38 percent of riders who also used foursquare said that the program makes riding BART "more fun." Twenty-three percent had earned the Train Spotter badge, and 7 percent were proud of telling the pollsters that they were mayors of a particular station. The most intriguing result, however, was the fact that 14 percent of BART riders who use foursquare said they ride BART more often because foursquare and BART together make riding fun.[2]

Like many other organizations finding success with LBS, BART tapped into a service that its customers—riders—were already using. Even before the program started, regular BART riders who were also foursquare users had become mayors of all 43 stations.

Trendsetters like Cal and BART are proving that foursquare has the potential to influence actions, incentivize behavior, and create more engaging relationships. But colleges and public transit agencies aren't the only organizations discovering the engagement potential of partnering with foursquare. America's most famous rodent is getting in the act.

A Groundhog Partners with foursquare

Punxsutawney is a small town in Jefferson County, Pennsylvania, that is famous for one of its iconic residents—a groundhog named Phil. Punxsutawney Phil has been forecasting the season's weather for 125 years (never mind that a groundhog lives only about six years—Phil is special). When he emerges from his hole, he either sees his shadow or he doesn't. On February 2, 2011, he did not see his shadow, which, according to folklore, meant an early spring. Never mind that Phil is right only about 40 percent of the time. It's the tradition, pomp, and events that attract visitors to Gobbler's Knob every year, waiting in bone-chilling weather for Phil to make his appearance. And it happens every single year, as any local news reporter will tell you (Bill Murray played a weatherman who had covered the event one too many times in the movie *Groundhog Day*).

About 7,000 people live in Punxsutawney, but on February 2, 2011, 28,000 shouted "It's Groundhog Day!" to their friends on foursquare. By doing so they unlocked a customized PA Groundhog Day badge, marking a one-day record for partner badges.

The PA Groundhog Day badge was just the latest foursquare promotion created by VisitPA.com, the tourism arm of the Commonwealth of Pennsylvania. The tourism bureau prominently features its foursquare partnership on its website, www.visitpa.com. The website is used as a traditional promotional vehicle to attract out-of-towners to the beautiful and historical places that Pennsylvania has to offer. But with foursquare, Pennsylvania tourism officials have discovered a way to engage tourists wherever they may be visiting in the state.

Polka, Food, and History

Punxsutawney Phil is just one reason to love Pennsylvania. The Keystone State is known for its history, sports teams, and food (chocolate, ketchup, hoagies, cheese steaks, and other regional foods are associated with this state in one way or another). But polka? Yes, Pennsylvanians love their polka, and so Pennsylvania became the first state to offer a foursquare polka badge.

To unlock the PA Retail Polka badge, users must follow a three-step process:

1. Sign up for foursquare, and download the app to your mobile phone.
2. Follow "VisitPA" on its foursquare venue page (http://four square.com/visitpa).
3. Check in to three eligible locations (from approximately 40 venues across the state).

One of the eligible locations is the King of Prussia Mall located—where else—in King of Prussia, Pennsylvania. A visitor to the state who uses foursquare might come across the most popular tip about the mall, posted by VisitPA: if you need retail therapy, the Dr. is in. The King of Prussia Mall is the largest shopping mall on the East Coast, home to more than 400 stores and restaurants. Warm up the plastic and have a Cinnabon for us!

The Polka badge is just one of three partner badges that the state uses to engage visitors. Foursquare users can also unlock two other badges: users who check in to three "food"-tagged establishments, like the 9th Street Italian Market in South Philly, the Cashtown Inn in Gettysburg, or Yocco's, "The Hot Dog King," in Allentown, can earn the Shooflyer badge. History buffs can earn the exclusive 4 Score & 7 badge by visiting three historical sites, such as the Andy Warhol Museum in Pittsburgh, Independence Hall in Philadelphia, or the new Flight 93 National Memorial in Stoystown, which honors the everyday Americans who thwarted a terrorist attack.

The PA Office of Tourism (www.visitpa.com) serves as the official sponsor of the tourism bureau's foursquare program. "What surprised me was that we are still getting 800 to 1,000 followers a week, eight months after the launch,"[3] says

85

Richard Bonds, director of social media for the Pennsylvania Office of Tourism. "After the Groundhog Day promotion, we climbed to more than 50,000 followers on VisitPa's foursquare page (http://foursquare.com/visitpa). This tells me two things. First, the word is out that foursquare is a fun way to do interesting things, and second, foursquare continues to grow."

Pennsylvania's foursquare strategy has attracted branding exposure that might have exceeded its marketing budget. The information is also valuable to tourism officials. Marketers can see when and where visitors unlocked the badges, which offers valuable data on travel and tourism trends. The program also succeeded in attracting visitors to places off the beaten path, driving traffic to local retailers and restaurants in some of Pennsylvania's smaller, charming communities.

Convincing small businesses to partner with the tourist bureau wasn't always easy. "Some smaller businesses were initially resistant," said Bonds. "They were suspicious of having their venues added to the list, even though it was a program the tourist bureau initiated. We had to convince some owners that this would be a new way to drive traffic, with no cost attached."

Bonds says that foursquare helps Pennsylvania tourism officials accomplish several "engagement" goals:

- Get the word out that Pennsylvania is a fun, exciting, and versatile destination.
- Implant the brand VisitPA on a growing communications platform that by its nature enhances the travel experience.
- Enrich the tourism bureau's other social network channels.
- Expose visitors to places and things to do that they may have otherwise overlooked.
- Encourage partners, attractions, and businesses to use foursquare to reward and inform visitors.

Bonds says the mission of Pennsylvania's tourism bureau is to put the state on everyone's to-do list. "Our partnership with foursquare helps to accomplish our mission."

A Philly Burger Joint Turns a Snow Day into a Boom Time

One way to unlock the Shooflyer badge is to visit Philadelphia's famous burger joint PYT. In February 2011, Philadelphia was gripped by heavy snowstorms. On a particularly hard-hit day when most businesses were closed, owner Tommy Up had no problem packing his restaurant, even on a day when the city decided to suspend bus service.

Tommy Up runs PYT, a Northern Liberties burger joint that serves what you would expect from a Philly burger joint— beer and burgers. These aren't just any burgers, of course. Rachel Ray once stopped in for PYT's epic Korean Short Rib burger. You see, PYT is home to America's craziest burgers, including the Krispy Kreme burger, the Cheesesteak Pretzel Roll burger, and the Surf 'N Turf truffled lobster burger.

Up doesn't have much of an advertising budget, but with foursquare, he doesn't need it. He does not place ads in the weekly newspapers, nor does he hand out flyers. He used to, but he felt like he was hitting his head against the wall. Foursquare is so much easier, he says.

On a snowy day when the other restaurants were closed, Up sent a message to his foursquare followers and told them that anyone who arrived early to the restaurant would be able to take advantage of an open bar. It worked too well. By 1:00 P.M. so many people had checked in that Up went into his foursquare merchant account and removed the offer. Up had turned a blizzard into one of the hottest days of the winter season. But Up's success did not happen overnight. Real engagement takes time—on any social media platform, including foursquare.

During the time I was writing this book, I met with executives at SanDisk, the world's leader in flash memory products. SanDisk pioneered flash cards for digital cameras, but today most of its revenue is derived from the mobile category of electronics—tablets, laptops, and smartphones. It sells cards directly to consumers but also sells memory (NAND flash) directly to smartphone manufacturers who embed the flash products in their phones—those pictures and videos you take on your phone must get stored somewhere.

SanDisk executives gave me an explanation of where smartphones fall on the "mobile continuum." People use tablets or netbooks largely for *consumption*: reading e-books, visiting websites, and reviewing documents and e-mail. On the other end of the scale, people use laptops for content *creation*: creating PowerPoint presentations, editing video, and recording podcasts. Smartphones sit in the middle. People use their smartphones for *engagement*: making calls, sending texts, uploading text and photos to Facebook, and interacting with friends and businesses.

By definition *engage* means to attract, involve, and retain one's attention. Engagement has been the name of the game for as long as businesses have existed. Today foursquare offers a new and novel way to engage your customers using the tool, the smartphone, they use for that very purpose.

UNLOCK THE POWER

♦ **Think differently about who your customers are.** Be specific about who you are choosing to engage on foursquare. A college campus must engage donors, students, and parents who are footing the bill. A public transit agency engages riders who want to save time on their commute, save on gas, or reduce air pollution. A tourism bureau engages visitors who are already in the state, out-of-towners deciding where to go for their next vacation, or people who live in the area but have yet to discover new and interesting places nearby. Each of the businesses or organizations featured in this chapter are successfully engaging their customers or supporters on foursquare because they are specific about who their customers are and they tailor promotions to meet the needs of those customers. Every brand has a unique story to tell. Tell your story in a way that is consistent with your unique position in the neighborhood, community, city, or state.

◆ **Contact foursquare directly for custom badges.** Foursquare keeps a tight lid on the badge process, including the price for creating a custom badge, which it does not disclose. Foursquare is selective for good reason—there's value in scarcity. If thousands of brand-sponsored badges suddenly became available, the perceived value of earning those badges would drop. Foursquare and its partners want to continue to inspire users to take actions to unlock the badges.

◆ **Add value to people's lives.** Foursquare and other mobile marketing tools allow you to educate, inform, and entertain. All three components are essential to a successful campaign. Use foursquare to teach people something new about your business or their neighborhood, inform those users about unique offers, and have fun doing it.

CHAPTER 6

Superusers

> *Don't make the mistake of thinking that discounts attract onetime-only customers looking for a deal. They are extremely loyal and spread the word via their mobile network of friends.*

—**ADAM WALLACE,** Digital Media Director, Roger Smith Hotels

How to unlock the Super User badge
Check in 30 times in one month.

C ompetition is fierce in many industries, and the great global recession of the past few years hasn't helped, especially for companies in the areas of hospitality, tourism, or entertainment. Here are two stories of brands that have embraced foursquare and other social media tools to engage their visitors and to grow their businesses in a time of great economic challenge.

The Hotel That Social Media Built

📍 **ROGER SMITH HOTEL**
New York, New York

Most visitors to New York tend to stay at brands who have worldwide name recognition: Marriott, Hyatt, Sheraton, or Omni. How is a small boutique hotel expected to compete? The Roger Smith Hotel in Midtown Manhattan does so quite successfully, thanks to social media tools like Facebook, Twitter, and foursquare that allow it to extend its unique brand story to a massive network of people around the world. The Roger Smith Hotel is truly the hotel that social media built.

Roger Smith is a boutique hotel located in the middle of a thriving hotel district on the corner of Lexington and East 47th. Popular destinations such as Grand Central Terminal, the Chrysler Building, and United Nations Plaza are within five blocks. Extend the radius another few blocks, and you'll run into Central Park, Times Square, and the Empire State Building. Extend the radius 3,000 miles west, and you'll encounter a Seattle woman who wrote a flattering blog post about the hotel, its events, and its community of patrons. The woman had never been to the hotel nor had she ever visited New York, but she loved everything about it and was willing to share her "experience" with a broad network of friends.

Roger Smith has cultivated this broad network since 2006 when it first launched its blog, http://rogersmithlife.com. The blog is a place where Roger Smith can share stories—stories of its employees, activities, art exhibitions, musical events, and the experiences of the people who visit the hotel from around the world. Adam Wallace, director of digital marketing for the hotel, believes that all companies, not just hotels, must provide online content that goes well beyond the products they sell. "We started telling our story with videos on our blog. People could see that we were engaged in the music, art, and the culinary scene."[1]

Two years later, 2008, Roger Smith began to post its stories and videos to Facebook and a two-year-old platform called Twitter. Roger Smith was not the first hotel to have a Twitter account, but it soon became one of the most active hotels on the service. Above all, its Facebook and Twitter presence helped the hotel shift from broadcasting stories it had created to letting people share and contribute their own personal stories, content, and feedback. Once the connection was made online, Roger Smith's online presence exploded. "People began to see us as more than a hotel that put heads in beds," says Wallace. "We became part of the culture and the community."

Roger Smith made a choice to participate in the conversation, to share its stories, and to engage an audience beyond New Yorkers. According to Wallace, "Social media has resulted in a huge change in the way we market our hotel, getting people to think about us even before they book a trip to New York or an event. Nothing beats word of mouth, and now past, current, and future guests share stories and information through the networks. It started with our blog, then Facebook, Twitter, and now, foursquare."

Roger Smith does not use foursquare to offer specials, nor does it post tips. But it has become extremely valuable as a tool to spread the Roger Smith experience through word of mouth. "We tapped into a community of people who were already active foursquare users," says Wallace. "When people check in to an event at the hotel or in a room, or restaurant, or bar, they often share that check-in and their experience with their larger network of friends on foursquare, Facebook, and Twitter. When people come to town, they book rooms or events with us because they've already heard about us from their friends. That's powerful, and we've seen a phenomenal growth in people booking with us because they heard about us through social media."

Wallace and others at the Roger Smith actively court bloggers, social media experts, and mobile users who live in New York. No, they may not be booking rooms, but they are highly influential among their friends. As the word of mouth spreads, Roger Smith gets noticed by potential visitors all over the world. "We see a huge upside in those networks," says Wallace.

Wallace and his team track the popularity of foursquare and its integrated social media campaign by doing two things: asking event organizers where they heard about the hotel and offering 10 percent discount specials for customers who book through an online or mobile social network. Although Wallace will not release specific numbers due to competitive reasons, he did tell me that the rate of return from social media easily pays the expense of employing a full-time social media director "many times over."

"Why should other businesses be on foursquare at this early stage?" I asked Wallace.

"Because as smartphone use grows, so will location-based service [LBS]. It's important to be part of the wave early on. Get people to actively talk about your business online and to their mobile social networks. Foursquare is a great way to start the conversation. You might not have thousands of people checking in at your venue, but by initiating conversations with those who are, word of mouth will spread."

The real value of integrating foursquare with Facebook and Twitter is not because someone will drop in once to redeem a 10 percent off coupon. According to Wallace, the real value is unlocked when the patron shares his or her experience with a wider network. "We recently had a party here, and out of 100 people, 50 were checked in to foursquare. That was large enough for those users to earn a Swarm badge. Most of them automatically shared the fact with their Twitter followers," Wallace recounts. The thousands of people who saw those Twitter posts were not at the hotel, but they saw that their friends were. That's influence. That's the power of the word of mouth. That's the power of foursquare.

A Theme Park's Thrilling foursquare Ride

 SIX FLAGS
Dallas, Texas

Twenty-five million people a year visit one of 19 Six Flags theme parks in North America. They enjoy shows, live concerts, and roller coasters—the "baddest, fastest, and steepest" in the world. At the Six Flags Great Adventure in Jackson, New Jersey, riders on the Kingda Ka reach a speed of nearly 130 miles per hour and drop from a height of 418 feet. It's the tallest and fastest roller coaster in the United States. On the opposite side of the country, at the Six Flags Magic Mountain outside of Los Angeles, the Goliath lives up to its name with unique twists and turns and intense g-force acceleration.

The company runs these coasters, shows, and attractions at parks in the United States, Canada, and Mexico, and it keeps close tabs on the data they glean from visitors. They know that of those 25 million visitors, 90 percent desire to return. They know the average guest spends 8.55 hours at the park. And they knew that foursquare's rate of growth, especially among the park's visitors, was simply too great to ignore. "Everyone was talking about it. Its growth has been incredible,"[2] said

CHECKING IN

"Foursquare is new, fun, creative, interactive, and easy to use. Since the game aspect makes foursquare unique, have fun with your fans by playing to the game's strengths."

—ANGEL ARISTONE,
Director of Communications and Social Media, Six Flags

Angel Aristone, Six Flags director of communications and social media. "Foursquare has become one of the hottest trends on the Web and continues to build momentum. It presented yet another innovative way Six Flags could engage our social media fans."

Foursquare's mission—to encourage exploration and location sharing—fit perfectly with a destination venue like a theme park. The park decided to first experiment with the service in the summer of 2010. Fans of the Six Flags foursquare page who checked in at the same Six Flags theme park 10 times earned a customized Six Flags Funatic badge and were entered to win a 2011 Unlimited Exit pass. "An Unlimited Exit pass has never been offered in our 50-year history. We thought it was a great way to celebrate our 50th birthday in 2011," said Aristone.

The badge was available for fans to unlock through September 7, 2010. At the conclusion of the campaign, the mayor of each park in the Six Flags family was granted a 2011 season pass. Foursquare users who check in to Six Flags parks also receive valuable insider tips posted by Six Flags staff. Tips include:

- **Six Flags Great Adventure, Jackson, New Jersey:** On a clear day you can see both New York City and Philadelphia from the top of Kingda Ka.
- **Six Flags Great America, Gurnee, Illinois:** Have children measured at Guest Relations when you arrive. They will

receive a height wristband that they can show to the ride operator instead of having to be measured at each ride.

◆ **Six Flags Fiesta, San Antonio, Texas:** Some of the most overlooked parking spots are very close to the front entrance. These spots used to be marked as handicapped but are now regular parking.

Aristone says foursquare is different from other mobile social networking tools because of the added incentive of the game and the competition for points, badges, and mayorships. She compared it to offering a virtual loyalty program for their online, mobile, and digital fans. "The reaction was extremely positive," according to Aristone. "The promotion was a great incentive for our most dedicated fans and one that was truly exclusive. We became one of the top brands on foursquare and will definitely continue to use the software."

As with all social media, Aristone found it difficult but not impossible to measure the return on investment. Aristone says it's important that brands commit to emerging social media trends and to become the leaders. "Foursquare presents another unique way for Six Flags to engage fans while creating a virtual loyalty program. We know that we're making positive strides when we see our fans and followers continue to grow, even in our off-season. Both platforms—Facebook and foursquare—are extremely valuable to help us reach our core audience, and we will be active on both. But what separates foursquare from other social sites is the incentive of earnings badges, points, and mayorships. The competition offers something extremely unique to its users as well as the ability to share that experience with others."

Aristone is confident about the platform after seeing that Six Flags' social media fan base continues to grow even during the off-season. She and Six Flags remain committed to the early adoption of location-based tools to engage an increasingly mobile fan base. "Foursquare is the biggest success story in social media right now. Foursquare is new, fun, creative, interactive, and easy to use. We're having lots of fun and will continue to explore new ways to engage our fans."

97

UNLOCK THE POWER

- **Encourage sharing.** Word spreads very quickly on mobile social networks. Encourage your customers to share their experiences. Host a party, offer incentives for people to post a tip, or create specials that reward people for bringing their friends.
- **Be a leader.** Don't wait for case studies. Be the case study. You have nothing to lose.

CHAPTER 7

Create Rewards

> *When you're the mayor you might be the coolest person in the room for five minutes. Who doesn't want recognition? And on top of it, you're rewarding my loyalty.*
>
> —**NAVEEN SELVADURAI,** Cofounder, foursquare

asti D-Lite is a famed frozen dessert chain that is making social media history by rewarding loyal customers and encouraging them to share the love. Over its 20-year history, Tasti D-Lite has gained a cultlike following among its customers who enjoy its unique blend of dairy-based, soft-serve desserts that offer a low-calorie alternative to ice cream. Loyal customers like the dessert because it contains less of what they don't want—calories, fat, and carbs—and more of what they do want—creamy, delicious taste. Today the Tasti franchise has grown to more than 50 locations in more than one dozen states from New York to California.

It's hard to believe that a 20-year-old institution is leading the industry in mobile social networking, but Tasti is reinventing the loyalty business in a way that has left its competitors scrambling to figure out how it's being done. Foursquare is one-third of the answer.

Traditional Marketers Need Not Apply

B. J. Emerson, Tasti D-Lite's vice president of technology, readily acknowledges that he does not have a classic marketing or PR background. It hasn't hurt him or his company. In fact, it's allowed him to upend traditional marketing loyalty programs by seeing his customers through a new paradigm, reaching his customers where they are now and not where they were several years ago. "The spirit of what we are doing on Twitter, Facebook, and foursquare is very different from what classical marketers have been doing for years. We are not blasting our sales messages—big agendas don't translate well into the end customer's community,"[1] says Emerson. "The opportunity is tremendous, if you approach social media like a conversation and think creatively about how you can add value to followers."

So how did Tasti take advantage of this "tremendous" opportunity? It did so by rewarding its most loyal customers, connecting foursquare check-ins to a loyalty card, and giving its most loyal fans a way to share the Tasti experience with friends on their extended social networks.

Monitor, Mingle, and Measure

Tasti's foursquare story started before foursquare even existed. The company had been granting foursquare-style rewards on another social media platform—Twitter. Emerson heard about Twitter in May 2008. He wasn't sure how to take advantage of the platform—so he listened. He used search terms to listen to what Twitter followers were saying about Tasti and its products. Listening—or monitoring—existing conversations is the first step in Emerson's "Three M" social media strategy:

 ◆ monitor
 ◆ mingle
 ◆ measure

During Emerson's "monitoring" phase, he discovered an opportunity to "mingle." One afternoon a customer working in the Empire State Building posted a tweet—he had a craving for Tasti D-Lite but could not pull himself away from the office. The office worker expressed his frustration that the building's rules barred outside food deliveries. Emerson dived into the conversation and clarified that because Tasti was located *in the building,* it was exempt from the delivery restrictions. Emerson sent the customer a coupon via Twitter and also had Tasti deliver frozen quarts, pints, and a cake to the man's office. The customer was thrilled as were his colleagues. In one simple gesture via a social network, Tasti had built goodwill, raised awareness, and most likely created a new group of loyal fans who would share their enthusiasm with others on Twitter and Facebook. "We were doing location-based services before the technology existed," says Emerson. "We were just doing it manually on Twitter. I call it proactive gesturing."

In August 2009, Emerson discovered foursquare, or rather foursquare discovered him. Tristan Walker, foursquare's vice president of marketing, was actively encouraging brands to be part of foursquare's initial rollout. Tasti D-Lite would become part of the original 15 brands on the platform (today more than 250,000 local merchants are on the platform). Emerson said Walker's pitch appealed to him for three reasons:

1. It was free.
2. It redefined "customer loyalty" because it gave customers an opportunity to share their love with their friends.
3. It was free.

Tasti became a launch partner and offered a simple special—a discount on a cup or cone for checking in. According to Emerson, the parlors that participated in the trial and offered the special saw an increase in foot traffic. But something much more powerful was about to happen.

Around the same time as its foursquare experiment, Tasti was deploying a new loyalty card program across all its franchises. Tasti was implementing a technology upgrade so all locations would use the same hardware and software, giving customers one loyalty card that could be used across all locations. Once the loyalty cards were connected with foursquare, it became a wildly successful rewards program. You see, foursquare created a special API (application programming interface) that let Tasti customers connect the loyalty card with their personal Twitter or Facebook accounts. "So really for us, it was the perfect storm," says Emerson. "All the right players and technology and opportunity came together at the right time, and we were able to execute on it."

Tasti made it easy for customers to join the program. Tasti customers register their TreatCard on the MyTasti website (http://mytasti.com) and optionally enable their Twitter and foursquare accounts to automatically send tweets or shouts to their friends whenever they check in and earn points. Customers accrue 1 point for each dollar spent. Once

CHECKING IN

"The spirit of what we are doing on Twitter, Facebook, and foursquare is very different from what classical marketers have been doing for years."

—**B. J. EMERSON,** Vice President of Technology, Tasti D-Lite

they reach 50 points, they can redeem a free cup or cone. Integrating loyalty cards with foursquare users and their social networks proved to be a powerful marketing proposition for Tasti D-Lite.

Two Million Reasons for Using foursquare

Now for the million-dollar question—did the foursquare program work? Emerson will give you two million reasons for why it did. By connecting the loyalty card, foursquare check-ins, and customers' Twitter and Facebook accounts, Tasti D-Lite garnered 2.2 million online social media impressions in 2010. It accumulated millions of social impressions because 28 percent of Tasti's loyalty cardholders chose to enable their social networks, linking their foursquare check-ins to Twitter and Facebook. This means that every time they check in, become mayor, or earn a reward, the information is shared among hundreds and in many cases thousands of friends and followers. We all know that a friend's recommendation is the most powerful form of marketing available. The average Tasti D-Lite loyalty-card holder has more than 90 friends or followers on their social networks. Those followers are hearing about Tasti directly from another friend, sometimes multiple times a week. The Tasti story hasn't changed, but the tool it uses to share its story most certainly has.

A huge increase in social networking impressions is just one result of the foursquare campaign. Tasti's loyal customers also spend more money. According to Emerson, the average sale across all franchises in Tasti's network is up 12 percent over nonloyalty customers. And the investment was minimal.

Since the infrastructure was already in place for the loyalty program to take effect, franchise owners were spending 10 cents on the card. Foursquare did the rest. The foursquare campaign has also helped Tasti reach a new demographic. Most Tasti customers are female (70 percent). At the time of this writing, the foursquare demographic was 60 percent male (this will change as it becomes more mainstream). But for Tasti D-Lite, the program allows them to reach outside their typical demographic. Figure 7.1 shows how the gender data is displayed on Tasti's dashboard. (Note: this image represents

FIGURE 7.1

This Tasti D-Lite foursquare dashboard displays a sample franchise's gender outreach.

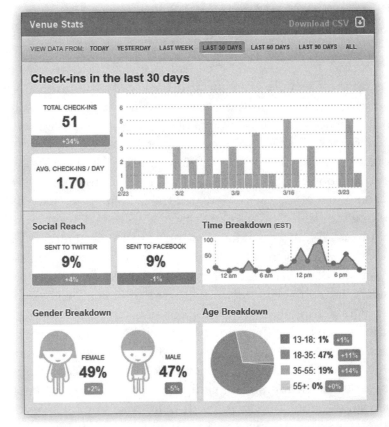

what a Tasti franchise owner can see on foursquare's dashboard and does not reflect the aggregate data across all of Tasti's locations.)

According to Emerson, the program just keeps giving because Tasti now has access to data it never had before foursquare, offering unparalleled insight into consumer behavior: where their customers shop, what they buy, their names, their social profiles, their average sale at Tasti stores, their points, their badges, their friends, and so on.

Foursquare's free manager tools include an analytics dashboard that provides Emerson and Tasti's franchise owners with more valuable data about their customers than just gender breakdown. The information also includes:

+ total check-ins (per day, week, or past 30, 60, or 90 days)
+ social reach (percentage of customers linking to Twitter and Facebook)
+ gender breakdown
+ age breakdown
+ time breakdown (when most check-ins occur)
+ top visitors (including mayor's first name and photo)

"With this kind of information, we can do more to target our customers and offer even more creative rewards," says Emerson.

Shortly before I first met Emerson in 2010, Pew Research came out with a study that showed "only" 4 percent of adults were using a location-based service like foursquare. Emerson thought the survey was deeply flawed. For starters, the survey was taken when foursquare was still in its infancy. Also, Facebook Places, a popular geolocation feature, had yet to be released. Facebook Places legitimized the check-in trend and helped raise foursquare's profile (foursquare had a record number of new users on the day Facebook Places was introduced and doubled its total number of users within six months). Third, and most troubling to Emerson, the survey polled "online adults" by phone. It did not take into account whether these adults use smartphones or mobile apps. If researchers had polled active smartphone users, the data would surely have been different. For example, Emerson has learned that 18 percent of Tasti's customers are four-square users. If Pew researchers had asked his customers, the research would have made the front page. Imagine: 18 percent of one brand's customers are using a new mobile social app that, at the time, was less than two years old. Equally as impressive, Emerson has learned that more than 60 percent of those foursquare users "enable" one social network. In other words, they link their foursquare check-ins to either Twitter or Facebook. About one-quarter of Tasti's foursquare customers link to two networks.

As more users join the foursquare community and share their Tasti experience with their friends, the chain remains top of mind when it comes to people's purchasing decisions. Figure 7.2 shows the check-in stats for several Tasti locations, so that Tasti managers can see the frequency of check-ins per venue location and develop specials based on these data. (Again, this is just a snapshot of one moment in time and is

FIGURE 7.2

Tasti D-Lite managers can watch the check-in status per venue location.

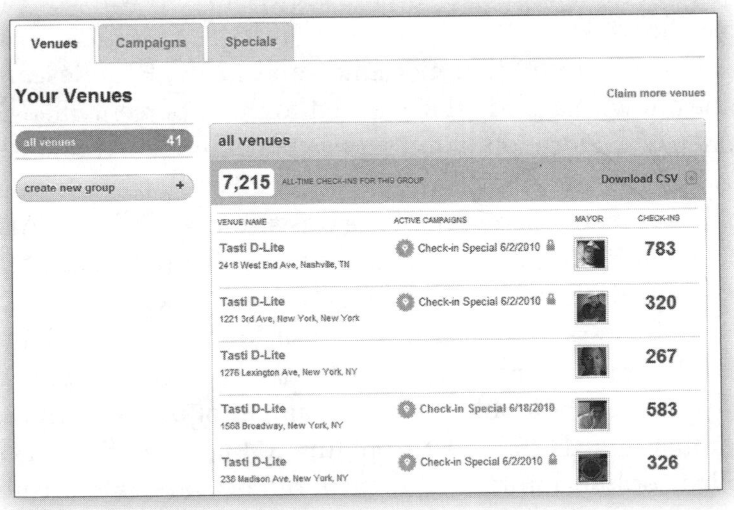

"Think creatively. There are plenty of opportunities to use foursquare to bridge the gap between the physical and the virtual worlds. Some companies are putting up digital displays in store that shows the foursquare mayor. Find a way to recognize the mayor in a public way. Why not put up a sign or even a chalkboard with the current mayor's name on it? Thank the people who frequent your business and encourage them to tell their friends."

—**B. J. EMERSON,** Vice President of Technology, Tasti D-Lite

not representative of all Tasti locations.) For Tasti's customers, they simply check in and reap the rewards. Now that's a frozen treat that will melt their hearts.

107

Redefining Customer Loyalty

Mobile social networks like foursquare are redefining customer loyalty. "It costs seven times more to acquire a new customer than it does to retain an existing one,"[2] says Tristan Walker, foursquare's vice president of business development. "And studies have shown that 20 percent of your customers contribute to 80 percent of sales. In that case, you need to focus on the 20 percent—rewarding and engaging them in the best way possible."

Who is a loyal customer? "Many people think of loyalty as punching a card to get something for free. That's not loyalty," says Walker. "I go to the same café every day without getting a 'deal' or a discount. But when I walk in, they say 'Hi, Tristan!' They also have my tea prepared just the way I like it. That inspires real loyalty and I share that experience with my friends. With foursquare, we're replicating that nostalgic experience."

My wife and I once enjoyed dinner at Spago in Beverly Hills—Wolfgang Puck's flagship restaurant. It's a two-star Michelin restaurant, so the food is excellent. But the most memorable part of the dinner was watching Mr. Puck himself greet patrons in the expansive dining room that is adjacent to a glass-enclosed kitchen where diners can see the chefs work their magic.

When Puck came out, the entire restaurant started buzzing as he shook hands, kissed, and hugged the diners. I thought to myself, *there's no way he's coming to our table. Those people must be regulars.* It's not surprising that a celebrity chef would come out of the kitchen to schmooze with his famous diners. But I was completely surprised and impressed to see Puck spend the next 30 minutes chatting with everyone at every table. And this place was packed. He stopped by our table, greeted us, shook our hands, asked us if we were there for a special occasion (it was an anniversary), and how we liked the meal. He was very charming and made us feel as special as the Hollywood power couples who were clearly in the room.

I learned something about customer service that night at Spago. Successful business owners treat everyone like royalty. But unless you're willing to greet each and every patron each and every day, a mobile location marketing tool like foursquare replicates the experience—not entirely, of course, but it's close, and the more personal you can make it, the better.

The Psychology of the Loyal Customer

Loyalty programs that are designed to get you to stick with a particular coffee shop, restaurant, retailer, or airline work by giving you perks. They work because of how your mind works. Psychologists who study loyalty programs say they provide a powerful motivator—the human mind enjoys minor accomplishments such as accruing points. An airline passenger might balk at spending $40 at the gate for the privilege of being the first to board, but you might spend $40 more for a flight where your loyalty membership card rewards you by letting you board first.

Psychologists will tell you that the human brain also likes routine. You might have a bedtime routine like brushing your teeth followed by reading a book. If your routine is disrupted, you might feel off-kilter. Loyalty programs operate on the same psychology, forcing you to develop habits that are tough to break. The more you participate, the closer you are to being rewarded, and your habit—or routine—gets cemented. That's why 9 out of 10 big-box retailers have loyalty cards. Loyalty programs work.

Loyal customers tend to spend more money when they redeem their points. The principle behind this effect is the concept of "found money." Let's say you accrued enough points to redeem a $50 gift certificate to a restaurant. Chances are high that you will bring someone along and spend even more money than you otherwise would have. You and your friend might spend $150. Subtract the $50 certificate, and the restaurant still comes out ahead. This is in addition to the money you spent to accrue the points in the first place, money that you might not have spent at the restaurant if you had no incentive to return.

Foursquare rewards work in much the same way and apply the same psychological principles that have made loyalty programs a standard practice across many industries. But as Tasti D-Lite has proven, check-in rewards have the potential to engage customers and encourage loyal behavior on a much deeper level than traditional loyalty programs. Why? It's called *gamification*.

Turning Life into a Game

Many business professionals initially dismiss social media networks, especially at the early stages, because they just don't understand the appeal. It's a dangerous attitude to have in the digital age. Who would have thought that 90 million people would be competing with their friends on Facebook to grow virtual vegetables and raise cows on a game called FarmVille? Many people spend several hours a day managing their virtual farms. You might think it's crazy, but plenty of people love it and FarmVille's success has helped the game maker, Zynga, generate $600 million in annual revenue.

How many people dismissed Twitter as a joke because they didn't understand why anyone would care that you had a latte this morning? Those who had that attitude missed the virtual boat. Twitter now has more than 100 million accounts, and more than 78 percent of small businesses are using Twitter to have conversations with their customers. Many of those small businesses, however, jumped on the platform well after their competitors were firmly entrenched on Twitter. In other words, they waited because they did not understand it or thought it was silly.

I came across a humorous blog post about the four stages of Twitter. Stage one was the complete inability to understand Twitter. The second stage was trying (and failing) to enjoy Twitter because you were rambling about the weather to a handful of followers. In stage three users finally begin to enjoy Twitter, as their popular posts get retweeted and they gain more followers. And of course, stage four was complete addiction.

I think foursquare and the checking-in trend follows a similar pattern as Twitter, both among users and popular media covering it. During the seven months I spent researching the topic and conducting interviews, the tone of the articles about foursquare in the mainstream media changed significantly. Writers who admitted that they didn't "get it" at first had become full-fledged evangelists, telling business owners that foursquare should be considered as an essential component of their social media strategy.

Foursquare is growing at a faster rate than Twitter did at similar stages. There's no telling if that growth rate will continue—but at one million new users a month, there is a good likelihood that foursquare will continue to build awareness.

So when it comes to checking in, you'll be making a big mistake if you check out without giving it a chance.

You might not care about becoming the virtual mayor of anything. But your customers do, and that's all that should matter. In its first six months, foursquare grew from 200 initial users to one million, and users checked in to 380 million establishments in one year. Chances are good that one of those establishments was yours. What are you doing to reward those customers who are competing for the mayor title?

Foursquare is popular because it adds game mechanics to a platform originally intended to let a group of friends in New York City keep tabs on each others' whereabouts. The gamification of mobile social media networks is just another way for people to keep score. As humans we love to count—we count how much money we've made or saved, how many fish we caught, how many miles we've run, how many readers visited our blogs, and so on. We count and compare. Sociologists call it acquiring social capital. Foursquare simply offers a new way to count and compare achievements, with points, leaderboards, badges, and mayorships. In addition, we can compare and brag about our achievements with our friends on Twitter and Facebook. By helping your customers earn rewards, compete, and share that experience with their friends, you win as well.

The game aspect of foursquare appeals to people of all ages. My wife, Vanessa, told one of her friends about foursquare but didn't think the woman would become an active user because, frankly, she fell outside the "demographic." Vanessa's friend, Cathy, is 64 years old and is not an active user of other online social media tools. But Vanessa had a theory. She thought it would appeal to Cathy because Cathy is social—she enjoys going out, traveling, and discovering new places. Vanessa was right. Within two weeks of joining foursquare, Cathy had acquired nine badges and five mayorships. Cathy had even earned the Crunked badge. Vanessa turned to me and said, "My 64-year-old friend got crunked before I did!" Foursquare had turned life into a game—a game that Vanessa and I were determined to win.

The Night I Got Crunked

They say you never forget your first time. Like most four-square users, my wife and I have never forgotten the first night we got crunked. You've never been crunked? It's a lot of fun, actually. The foursquare Crunked badge is earned by a user who checks in to four different venues in one night. We were meeting some friends for dinner in San Francisco and decided to hit some hotspots in the Union Square area including the Ghirardelli chocolate store and a very popular Italian restaurant. Upon our fourth check-in, we both received e-mails at the same time notifying us of our achievement. We smiled, laughed, and gave each other a high five. Silly? You bet it is. But as a business owner you need to understand this behavior. We weren't the only ones who got crunked that night. Every minute of every day, somewhere in the world someone is getting crunked and sharing the experience with his or her Twitter and Facebook friends. Again, you might think it's silly. You might not give a rip about checking in and earning a badge, but *your customers do,* and the better you understand this powerful reward mechanism, the more effectively you can use foursquare to create innovative marketing programs. If you still don't get it, that's fine. Your competitors will.

If you still need to be convinced of the potential of checking in, meet a Baltimore native nicknamed Spam. He's a four-square superuser who has gone by the nickname of Spam well before e-mail was invented. Spam told me that the gaming aspect of foursquare—competing for mayorships and earning badges—is a lot more addictive than he expected it would be. "I find myself making decisions on where to eat, shop, and even where to buy my gas, depending on whether I have a mayorship to defend or if I'm trying to earn a mayorship. In fact, I intentionally make smaller purchases at a grocery store or a gas station just so I can check in more often."[3] Spam lives in Baltimore, has checked in more than 3,000 times, and holds 25 mayorships. Spam has more than 300 friends on foursquare, 1,400 followers on Twitter, and 800 friends on

Facebook. He's sharing his check-ins. He's sharing his badges. He's sharing his mayorships. Any establishment that rewards Spam for his loyalty will be rewarded itself as it becomes recognized among Spam's friends and social networks.

Where Rewards Fit on the Hierarchy of Needs

Early critics of foursquare dismissed the gaming aspect of the platform because they didn't understand why anyone would want to be the mayor of a venue, especially if no freebies or discounts came with the title. Skeptics were more numerous when foursquare had 50,000 users but became less vocal as foursquare attracted a million users, and another million, and many more millions. What the critics needed was a psychology lesson brought to them by Abraham Maslow, the guru of the self-actualization movement.

You've heard of Maslow before—if you haven't, you are probably familiar with his theory on motivation and the hierarchy of needs. Simply put, as human beings we need air, food, water, sleep, and shelter. Those needs are the foundation of the pyramid. We can't live without them. But when our basic needs are met, we crave things like friendship, family, respect, and recognition. We want to belong to a group, and we want to be recognized for our achievements.

Merchants who successfully leverage the foursquare platform and reward mayors are tapping into a deep-seated psychological need for recognition and achievement. They are inadvertently helping people become self-actualized! In this final stage of Maslow's hierarchy of needs, people are encouraged to reach their full potential. You might be asking yourself, *how can rewarding a mayor with a free drink possibly lead to self-actualization?* The free drink might not reach the level of self-actualization but instead satisfies Maslow's esteem need, the need for status, recognition, and attention. But what if a venue could use foursquare to encourage you to be healthier and in better shape? That's exactly what one fitness chain did to reward its loyal customers and help them advance through the hierarchy of needs.

24-Hour Fitness is a hugely successful fitness club with more than 400 locations around the United States and more than three million members. It created a simple foursquare special. Anyone who checks in receives a $3 discount on any Scosche product (the fitness chain stocks items for mobile devices like earphones or phone covers). Customers can redeem the discount at the front desk when they purchase the product. The big reward is reserved for the mayor. The mayor of participating locations is entitled to one free personal training session.

Prices will vary, but the typical fee for a personal training session at 24-Hour Fitness is about $50. Offering a free training session was a smart move. Personal training is addictive. A good trainer shows you new exercises, provides nutritional advice, and in many cases pushes you harder than you could possibly push yourself. A free personal training session is significant. Good rewards encourage competition. When an enticing reward is combined with a naturally competitive group of customers like those found in a fitness club, it can be a magical formula for a business. I know people who work out more often and check in more frequently to become mayor so they can work out even harder in a free personal training session. Got it? If not, that's OK. Your customers get it, and as a business owner that's all that matters.

The Story of a True Super Mayor

My wife, Vanessa, has earned a Super Mayor badge. That means she holds down at least 10 mayorships at once on foursquare. She checks in nearly everywhere she goes, despite the fact that she doesn't get always get rewarded for it. We live in a small town 50 miles east of San Francisco. As of this writing, foursquare is catching on with locals, but few local merchants are leveraging the full power of its reward mechanism—with the exception of a few forward-thinking national brands. By the time you read this, local businesses will probably be far more active in our town. But despite the lack of physical rewards from the establishments she visits, Vanessa still checks in. She does so to keep her titles. It's addictive. But although the psychological motivation is enough to keep her going back for now, it could wear thin over time. Now imagine that those businesses actively embrace her as their mayor and reward Vanessa for her loyal behavior. The real power of foursquare could be unleashed by encouraging Vanessa to return and sparking a competition between her friends and other foursquare users. Here are 10 of the locations where Vanessa has earned mayorships and some ideas on how these businesses could potentially reward her loyalty.

1. Express Fitness

This gym is one of several fitness facilities in Pleasanton. It doesn't have all the bells and whistles of a larger gym, but it has clean equipment, televisions, classes, and best of all for us, a kids center.

115

- ◆ **Mayor's Reward Idea:** Mayor is guaranteed a spot in Zumba or favorite class. Just show this special and get in line!
- ◆ **Why it would work:** This gym is missing an opportunity. 24-Hour Fitness just built a mega-gym nearby, and some Express members have left to join the new facility. Some of the members at Express complain that classes fill up too quickly. Vanessa can't always show up one hour early, especially with two small kids. With a unique mayor's reward, Express can engage a growing group of mobile young professionals who are socially connected. It would also spark a competition among members who already compete to be early in line.

2. Bibiane

An amazing bakery located in the heart of downtown Pleasanton, Bibiane is known for its artisan breads, cakes, and cookies.

- **Mayor's Reward Idea:** Mayor gets a free baguette, croissant, or cupcake (limit one per day).
- **Why it would work:** Most people who walk into Bibiane for one small item walk away with a larger order than they anticipated. The owners do a good job of making sure the smell of the freshly baked bread comes wafting to the front of the store. But they do acknowledge that given their location is tucked behind some other establishments, it is difficult for new customers to discover them. This promotion would reward Vanessa for her loyalty, persuade her to make even more purchases, and more important, spark a competition among Vanessa's friends who also frequent the bakery.

3. Gourmet Works

A downtown Pleasanton store specializing in gourmet foods, chocolate, fudge, and gifts.

- **Mayor's Reward Idea:** For the mayor, we take off an additional 20 percent on all purchases. Mayors also get a free truffle upon checkout.
- **Why it would work:** The store is known for its signature truffles, so getting one free becomes an incentive to buy something else just to get a truffle. Since the store does a good job of changing its inventory to reflect the season or holiday, Vanessa drops in several times a month (it's one of her favorite places to buy gifts). Sometimes she buys something. Sometimes she doesn't. A 20 percent discount is sizable enough to encourage Vanessa (or the mayor) to make a purchase instead of leaving the store empty-handed. Throw in a truffle, and the store has guaranteed a sale.

4. Berry Patch

A downtown main street arts and crafts store that features handcrafted pieces from local vendors.

- **Mayor's Reward Idea:** Mayor receives 20 percent off all purchases. All other customers receive 10 percent off mayor's "favorite artists."

♦ **Why it would work:** This promotion would create buzz among the store's customers and reinforce the store's mission to feature local artists. Each artist is featured in a section of the store. They could add a "foursquare mayor's" section and offer an added enticement of a 10 percent discount. This would bring awareness to the artists, reward the mayor for loyal patronage, and get other customers talking about a new and unique mobile platform.

5. High Tech Burrito

A small Bay Area chain serving fresh, healthy burritos, wraps, and salads.

♦ **Mayor's Reward Idea:** Free burrito on Friday for the mayor! Every Friday, the mayor of each High Tech Burrito location gets a burrito of their choice. It's our way of saying thanks and to help you kick off the weekend.

♦ **Why it would work:** This promotion would work because it encourages the mayor to visit the restaurant more often during the week to retain the mayor title. Since our office is across the street, I would join my wife when she eats there and probably for Free Burrito Friday as well. Even if she has only the burrito and a drink, I would order an entire lunch (in our minds it would feel like "buy-one-get-one free"). And once again, it would stoke competition among local diners, many of whom are very fond of the chain.

117

6. Quiznos

A large national quick-serve restaurant chain known for its tasty subs, soups, and salads.

♦ **Mayor's Reward Idea:** Mayor gets a free bag of chips and a drink with every sub purchase.

♦ **Why it would work:** Most people don't order just a sub sandwich from Quiznos. I often see diners with chips and a drink. By adding something extra that complements their meal, diners will have even more incentive to check in more often to become mayor.

7. Tiffany's Dance Academy

A small Bay Area chain of dance studios specializing in jazz, tap, and ballet for children.

- ◆ **Mayor's Reward Idea:** The mayor receives a 25 percent discount on monthly dance instruction.
- ◆ **Why it would work:** Parents pay a monthly fee for classes. The best incentive would be a reduced rate on their classes. Ten percent is OK, but a larger discount would create even more competition among the parents, many of whom are younger, tech savvy, and on their smartphones while their kids are in class. The studio would be reaching those parents right where they already are—on their phones outside the studio.

8. Towne Center Books

An independent local bookstore.

- ◆ **Mayor's Reward Idea:** Mayor gets 40 percent off each purchase (limited to once a day).
- ◆ **Why it would work:** Forty percent is an enticing discount. It's a little more than Amazon.com, and since a customer would have to show his or her phone to the cashier to buy the book in-store, the customer would save on shipping as well. The store has a large selection of books, so a local customer would be encouraged to shop locally instead of online. Plus, if other customers are like Vanessa, they feel good about supporting local merchants and the mayorship gives them another incentive for doing so.

9. U.S. Post Office

The Pleasanton branch of the U.S. Post Office. We send out so much material as part of our business that the clerks know my wife's name and the names of our kids, too.

- ◆ **Mayor's Reward Idea:** Mayors get their own dedicated line at this post office. Check in and skip the wait!

+ **Why it would work:** What's the biggest frustration at the post office? Lines, of course. Just as frequent fliers get their own dedicated lines at some airports, allowing the four-square mayor to cut to the front would create an enticing perk.

10. Rick's Picks

This store specializes in everyday deals on a wide variety of products, including arts and crafts, kitchen accessories, candles, books, toys, and other items. The deals are significant enough to encourage Vanessa to check in frequently, if only to see what's new.

+ **Mayor's Reward Idea:** Mayors get 10 percent off the pick of their choice!
+ **Why it would work:** This place is all about discounts. That's why people shop there. An extra 10 percent discount on an item that is already discounted 50 to 60 percent is a significant enticement and would stoke competition among budget-conscious shoppers.

119

These rewards for the foursquare mayor do not exist . . . yet. But they could easily be set up—for free. There's absolutely nothing for the establishment to lose. Rewards are only going to grow as more businesses discover the power of four-square to engage their loyal customers. Those companies who are not engaging the mobile user are missing a tremendous opportunity right under their nose. During one trip to New York City I stumbled upon a taqueria that had 5,700 customers who had checked in 10,000 times. The mayor had checked in 16 times in the previous 30 days. Despite this momentum, no one new had claimed the venue and no specials were being promoted—to newbies or the mayor. That's a missed opportunity. At the Museum of Modern Art in New York, more than 28,000 people had checked in a total of 56,000 times. Yet at the time the museum was offering no specials, no rewards, and no tips. Another missed opportunity.

For small businesses especially, foursquare has leveled the playing field. Now that small business owners can compete with larger competitors for mobile customers, they are limited only by the bounds of their creativity. Yet at the time of this writing most of the foursquare rewards in my nearby vicinity are being offered by national brands (Starwood, RadioShack, Chili's, etc.). Those brands are doing a great job, but you can be doing the same—for free.

When it comes to location-based marketing, small businesses have one big advantage over the big boys—speed. We all know how long it can take for a major brand to make a decision about any marketing initiative, mobile or otherwise. They have to schedule endless meetings to get buy-in from every level in the organization. As a small business owner, you can begin offering a creative foursquare reward for your mayor in less time than it takes for a large company to schedule the first of its 20 meetings on the topic.

There is no excuse for not participating in the mobile social networking revolution. Your customers are already using location-based check-in tools on their smartphones. They are getting more comfortable with the idea of checking in to share their location with their friends. They are having fun playing the game and exploring their city. Now they want to be rewarded for their loyalty, and it will cost you nothing to do so.

UNLOCK THE POWER

♦ **Feel your customers' pain.** If you manage a restaurant that is known for its hour-long lines on weekends, then it makes sense to create a reward structure that has meaning for your customers. Give the mayor special status so he or she can cut to the front of the line. The better you know your customers, the more creatively you can tailor a reward to entice them. If you're the manager of Express Fitness, then you need to know that people complain about the limited slots available for the free classes. The more you learn about your customers and their challenges, the better equipped you will be to set up an effective foursquare reward promotion.

* **Treat your mayor like royalty.** Create a unique reward for your most loyal foursquare customer—the person who has checked in the most times in the previous 60-day period. Don't shrink from offering a great reward for their loyalty—a reward that will stoke the competitive fire in your other customers.

* **Promote and publicize your rewards.** Foursquare users will talk about your rewards if they are worth talking about. But you must promote your specials as well. Promote your rewards through the channels that you already use to speak to your customers: Facebook, Twitter, blogs, ads, or in your establishment. Foursquare will also send you window stickers after you claim your venue, much like the Yelp stickers you see in the windows of restaurants. Use them. Put them on the front door or window of your venue. Foursquare users will be excited to see that you're engaging them and rewarding them for their loyalty. People who don't know about foursquare will start asking about it. Once they learn that they'll be rewarded for checking in to your place, they'll be hooked—to foursquare and your establishment.

121

CHAPTER 8

Super Mayors

 We wanted to do something that was going to generate some great buzz.

—**EDDIE DOPKIN,** Owner, Miss Shirley's Restaurant

How to unlock the Super Mayor badge
Hold the title of mayor at 10 different locations at the same time.

F oursquare cofounder Dennis Crowley believes that foursquare can be better at rewarding loyalty than anyone else. Merchants can now offer significant rewards to those people who visit their venues the most frequently. *Significant* is the key word. Crowley and I both agree that people don't want merchants to simply push coupons to their pockets when they walk by a coffee shop. Instead, the winning ticket is a service that tells you when a friend loves the coffee shop around the corner that you've never tried before. If that coffee shop, in turn, offers creative rewards, it stands a good chance of earning your patronage.

In this chapter you'll hear from two small business owners in completely different industries who are taking a creative approach to rewarding loyalty.

Where the Mayor Never Waits

MISS SHIRLEY'S CAFE
Baltimore, Maryland

Nobody leaves Miss Shirley's Cafe with an empty stomach, especially after breakfast. The menu includes 10 types of omelets, more than one dozen griddle cakes, and many other specialty dishes that have earned Miss Shirley's the designation of Maryland's Best Breakfast spot by *Food Network* magazine. It's also known for its gigantic portions. Patrons know better than to count the calories on the signature coconut-cream-stuffed French toast with mascarpone and candied bananas baked into the crust. Bring an appetite if you plan to eat there.

Eddie Dopkin, owner of Miss Shirley's, began offering a unique foursquare promotion to reward his best customers and to encourage even more visits by connecting with these loyal customers whenever they happened to be near the restaurant.

The unique promotion worked like this: anyone who checked in to Miss Shirley's and could prove he or she was the mayor by showing the phone to the hostess would be escorted to the front of the line during its popular breakfast, lunch, or brunch. According to the special: the mayor never waits for a table at Miss Shirley's.

The reward was popular among Miss Shirley's most loyal customers because with menu items like Shirley's Affair with Oscar (two beef fillets topped with asparagus, jumbo crab meat, hollandaise sauce, fried green tomatoes, and savory grits), the lines can be as enormous as the portions. "It's common for customers to have to wait anywhere from 45 minutes to an hour on weekends,"[1] says Dopkin. "Giving the mayor the ability to skip the line was a big deal. Not only did the promotion attract new people, it created a friendly competition among existing customers and encouraged them to come in more often. The buzz and hype over this unique promotion had a lot of impact on the restaurant."

Dopkin says the impact was noticeable. During the time of the promotion, Dopkin told me that Miss Shirley's saw a 420 percent increase in check-ins and an 18 percent increase in sales.

Miss Shirley's foursquare special was created by Baltimore marketing firm MGH. Ryan Goff, MGH's social media director, began experimenting with foursquare and wasn't all that excited by some of the specials he came across. Merchant specials were beginning to look the same: free drinks or 10 percent off. "We wanted to do something that would get some buzz,"[2] says Goff. "Once you get people talking, they want to participate. Offering 10 percent off your first check-in won't get people talking. We knew that a first-of-its-kind reward like letting a mayor go to the front of the line would get some good results."

Fortunately for Goff, the owners were also very receptive to the idea. Miss Shirley's issued a press release, and customers began spreading the word on their extended social networks. Bloggers started buzzing about it, and the *Baltimore Business Journal* and *Restaurant Week* covered the unique offer. "In the restaurant industry, it's rare for a campaign to be so successful without giving away something for free. We were extremely pleased with the results," says Dopkin.

Cutting to the front of the line was so inviting to some people, they actually tried to "cheat" the system. Some customers tried to cheat by checking in when they were not near the location. Those potential cheaters couldn't win, however, because foursquare gives businesses the option to oust a mayor if they believe the mayorship was not gained through a legitimate check-in. Sorry, cheaters!

Any business that launches a foursquare campaign or another mobile marketing promotion must train its staff. If you cannot properly educate your employees about your promotion, then please, for the sake of all your customers, do not run it! Dopkin held a staff meeting to explain foursquare to Miss Shirley's employees and to pass out images of what the promotion would look like on someone's phone. Dopkin even encouraged those staff members who were not using foursquare to sign up for a free account. Once they learned more about foursquare and the unique special, the staff was receptive and enthusiastic about educating their customers. If your

CHECKING IN

"To be successful at foursquare, you have to do something that will make people turn their heads. It has to be unique enough for them to say, 'Hey, I need to go to that place.' It has to be unique enough for those people to tell their friends about it as well."

—**RYAN GOFF,** Vice President,
Director of Social Media Marketing, MGH Baltimore

staff isn't behind the foursquare promotion—or any unique marketing idea— it won't work nearly as well as it should.

Miss Shirley's plans to do what it has always done: offer the best fried green tomatoes with grits that you'll find anywhere. But as the number of mobile customers in the Baltimore area continues to skyrocket, Miss Shirley's plans to offer even more specials to its menu—foursquare specials that stoke competition among its customers.

A Miami Realtor with a Flair for Rewards

 THE ORDOVER GROUP
Miami, Florida

Lori Levine Ordover has more than 30 years of experience in commercial and residential real estate. As a managing member of the Ordover Group, she oversees marketing and sales for high-profile residential developments in Miami and New York City. One of Ordover's properties is called the Marquis in Miami, a high-rise condominium complex overlooking Biscayne Bay.

Ordover's daughter, Jessica Kantor, introduced her to social media. Jessica is an avid technologist and social media user herself, so Lori trusted her daughter's instincts. Social media made sense to Lori. Condo developers had been trying to explore the link between online activities and offline results. Ordover began using foursquare as an extension of her own offline activities, such as cocktail parties. Ordover began holding MyPad open houses. These were events held in an open unit of the condo and were intended to target tech-savvy, single professionals, hip young couples, or retiring boomers. They were held in places like the Marquis Residences in Miami where owners have access to pools and restaurants on the property. People who checked in to open apartments were entered in an iPad giveaway.

Ordover says her social media strategy keeps the building top of mind for her social media followers, who she updates with regular posts about the tower. Ordover credits her social media efforts for at least one sale every two months. "We consider social media an important part of our outreach, just as important as placing ads in the newspaper or other marketing efforts. It's an essential part of our marketing campaign,"[3] she says.

Although her social media efforts were attracting new homeowners, Ordover wanted to do something truly unique, creative, and only available through foursquare. She created a unique incentive to motivate her brokers to sell condos at the Marquis Residences, a complex of nearly 300 ultraluxurious residential apartments and a five-star boutique hotel with some of the best views in Miami. Lori offered a foursquare mayor's special: any real estate broker who is mayor on a particular future date would get an extra 1 percent commission on a sale. For example, if the broker's commission was 3 percent, the mayor's commission would be bumped to 4 percent. In a development where high-end condos can range from $1 million to $2 million, the foursquare offer can mean an additional $10,000 to $20,000 for the mayor. According to Ordover, "It's a significant reward, it's fun, and it's amazing how much the brokers want to do it."

CHECKING IN

Think carefully about who your customers are and who you are trying to reach with your mobile marketing campaign. What would attract them and encourage their loyalty? Ordover's foursquare strategy rewarded the realtors who brought buyers to her properties, not the buyers themselves. Her campaign was perfectly tailored to solve their pain: how to generate more commissions.

Ordover says that social media is now just as important as newspaper ads, but one can't but wonder that, as her clients increasingly rely on their smartphones for information, Ordover's marketing mix might change to favor the twenty-first-century home buyer and real estate agent.

UNLOCK THE POWER

- **Turn heads.** Think bigger than simply offering a 10 percent discount or the same type of reward that you might offer on a standard coupon or mailer. If you want to generate buzz, you've got to turn heads.
- **Cure pain.** Thinking bigger doesn't necessarily mean offering bigger discounts. Miss Shirley's sparked a competition by curing a pain—waiting in long lines.

129

CHAPTER 9

Knock Out the Competition

"You go to where your customers are, and they are on places like foursquare."

—**EDWARD GILLIGAN,** Vice Chairman, American Express

n early 2011 a patron at AJ Bombers in Milwaukee, Wisconsin, was rewarded with 8,000 minutes of free food. That's a lot of fries, burgers, and beers. The customer won the free food for being the restaurant's 8,000th check-in on foursquare. AJ Bombers has become a poster child for the power of social media, and as you'll learn, location-based apps like foursquare have played a big role in its success (see Figure 9.1).

Although the restaurant is booming today, the outlook looked bleak in 2008 when Joe Sorge and his wife, Angie, were struggling small business owners. They owned four restaurants and a fifth, AJ Bombers, had just been returned to their possession because it wasn't doing well. Sorge credits social

FIGURE 9.1

AJ Bombers is a poster child for the power of social media.

media tools such as Twitter and foursquare for helping them dig out of their hole and create a thriving group of restaurants with AJ Bombers as its flagship. "I had to find a way to gain exposure without spending money,"[1] Sorge told me.

Where Everyone Knows Your (Twitter) Name

Sorge locked himself in an office for six months and learned everything he could about social media. He was determined to understand it, apply it, and educate his customers about it. Sorge knew he had an ace in the hole: tech-savvy customers who would appreciate his approach and tell their friends about it.

Sorge started with Twitter, leveraging the social media platform to build a community of people who were fans of social media. Customers began to feel welcome at AJ Bombers. A quote on the front door reminds them that they're home: "Where everyone knows your name. Well, at least your Twitter name." One blogger (and a loyal customer) said, "The best part of AJ Bombers is the people. Joe and his wife have created a restaurant that is a safe haven for those of us who have taken a liking to this new wonky world of social networking." When your customers consider your establishment a "safe haven," then you know you're on to something. But what Sorge was on to was even bigger than he could imagine.

Joe engaged his customers who were on Twitter and encouraged tweetups, gatherings, and events. Some events were planned months in advance, while others were spontaneous. Customers could log on to Twitter at any time to check on the happenings at their favorite burger joint.

Attracting a Swarm of Customers

Twitter was and continues to play a key role in AJ Bombers' success, but foursquare took Sorge's restaurant to another level—socially and financially. A custom entrée on the menu called the Barrie Burger made Sorge appreciate the full power of foursquare. The burger had been invented at AJ Bombers in honor of a Twitter user who was a fan of another restaurant that used an unusual blend of ingredients to cook up some wild recipes. Not to be outdone, Sorge and his team went into the lab and created a peanut butter and bacon cheeseburger (if you have to ask about the calories, it's not for you). Sorge featured the burger briefly on Twitter and left it at that. But despite very little active promotion, sales of the Barrie Burger continued to sizzle. Sorge soon learned why. His patrons were leaving tips about the burger on foursquare, and those tips became popular on AJ Bombers' foursquare venue page.

Sorge jumped into foursquare with both feet. AJ Bombers became the first foursquare venue to hold a Swarm party (foursquare users can unlock a Swarm badge when they are in the same venue as 50 other people who are also checked in). Sorge decided to attract enough local users to unlock the coveted Swarm badge. He promoted the event on his Twitter and Facebook pages. Sorge was pleasantly surprised. Not only had he attracted the 50 people necessary to unlock the badge, 100 additional customers showed up as well! The 150 foursquare users in his restaurant that day purchased enough beer and burgers to help the restaurant double its typical Sunday sales. The event's success lasted well after the celebration had ended. Sorge created a YouTube video of the event and posted pictures online at www.flickr.com/photos/ajbombers/.

One month later, on foursquare Day (April 16), Sorge invited foursquare users to his restaurant to unlock the I'm on a Boat badge party. The badge can be unlocked only if you're, well, on a boat. But few people know that it can also be unlocked by shouting "I'm on a boat" when you check in. Sorge invited a local sports and camping business to bring a kayak to the restaurant and to participate in the event. (Sorge tries to partner with other local businesses to raise more awareness for his events.) Customers would sit in the kayak, have their photo taken, check in, and shout "Happy fsq day. I'm on a boat!" The simple activity earned them a Boat badge and a Swarm badge.

Incentivize user-generated content. Reward your customers for telling your story through tips and photos. AJ Bombers once had a special that gave customers a free cookie in return for posting a tip on foursquare (the promotion led to hundreds of tips, most of which were highly favorable about the restaurant and its menu).

The I'm on a Boat event led AJ Bombers to post its best sales ever for a lunch crowd. The restaurant even had its longest wait times, as people were lined up outside the door before the event even started. "People like to participate in community events," says Sorge.

Loyalty Royalty

Sorge kept up the foursquare activities with badge parties and unique rewards. He even created an exclusive menu that only the mayor could order from. He calls it the Loyalty Royalty. It's a monthly menu that is created with input by the three customers who checked in the most on foursquare over the previous month. Only those loyal customers are allowed to order from the menu. One day a month the mayor's dishes are offered to all patrons. The purpose, of course, is to get everyone talking about the competition and sharing the event with their friends in the area.

Sorge's social media efforts worked so well the restaurant was the focus of a Travel Channel special called "Food Wars." The show's producers were looking for the best burger in Milwaukee and stumbled upon AJ Bombers thanks to its social media presence. The restaurant won the competition, which only propelled its growth even further.

"My goal was to enter the burger lexicon of Milwaukee," says Sorge. In other words, he simply wanted AJ Bombers to be part of the mix when someone asked, "Where can I go for a good burger?" In fact, Sorge outsmarted the competition in a big way. "For 10 years the best burger in the city had been prepared by a restaurant called Sobelman's (the restaurant owns the domain name milwaukeesbestburger.com). In 18 months, through our use of social media—Twitter, Facebook, and foursquare—we had gained an equal or greater amount of exposure than our competitor had received in the previous decade," says Sorge.

The people who patronize AJ Bombers are not all four-square experts. In addition to Sorge's role as restaurant owner, he's a social media educator as well. "My customers intro-duced me to foursquare, and I apply the same logic. We have turned our restaurant into a place of education. For example, when you search for a wireless signal at Bombers, our connec-tion is labeled 'Don't forget to check in on foursquare.' It came out of a desire to be fun, be creative, and involve my custom-ers. It's been so much fun that I genuinely forget that there is a business involved."

Who Wants Bombers in Their Town?

Sorge told me that all the awareness led to an investing partner who wants to introduce AJ Bombers to a national audience. "Everyone is familiar with the idea: build it and they will come. With social media and location-based market-ing, you develop a relationship with your customers first and then ask them what they want to see. We're using social media to choose our next cities. We're asking, 'Who wants Bombers in their town?' The people who scream the loudest will get it."

Here's the most intriguing part of Sorge's already amazing story, the part that every small business owner in American needs to know. Sorge says he did not spend a dollar on tra-ditional advertising. He and his wife were facing a deep recession in the restaurant business and needed to find the least expensive means of raising awareness. Sorge says he owes 100 percent of his success to social media. "And of that 100 percent, foursquare is responsible for up to 50 percent."

CHECKING IN

"Develop two-way relationships with your customers on social networks. This way they feel an ownership in your business. I work at social media every day. I respond to every single mention on Twitter. It's never not in front of me. I'm on my phone, my computer, or watching the live Twitter feed that we display in the restaurant."

—**JOE SORGE,** owner, AJ Bombers

Mobile Is Global

Sorge locked himself in an office for six months to learn social media. The work paid off, revitalizing his business and transforming his destiny. The good news is that you don't have to spend six months learning about mobile social media. The content you are holding will get you started. But it's not enough. Although the information is available to you, it's also available to your competitors. Winning takes commitment, dedication, and creativity. And that's where you can shine.

As a local merchant, business owner, or brand manager, you need to make a commitment to leveraging new social mobile media tools that will drive your company forward. Not everyone will share your commitment and that should be OK with you. Your competitors will wish they had shared your dedication in the early stages of the mobile social networking revolution.

Mobile platforms are reaching critical mass around the world, and social media is a big reason behind mobile's explosive growth. Kleiner Perkins' Internet strategist, Mary Meeker, forecasts that 50 percent of the population in developed markets will have smartphones by 2012.[2] In her opinion, that's the tipping point, catapulting smartphones into the mainstream.

137

TABLE 9.1

TASKS PERFORMED BY SMARTPHONE USERS

Type of Task	Percentage Spent on Task
Social networking, games, and utilities	47
Telephone (phone calls, messaging)	32
Web apps	12
Mail apps	9

That means more and more of your customers will be using them in all parts of the world. Those customers won't be using smartphones just to make phone calls and send instant messages. Table 9.1 lists the percentage of time the typical smartphone user spends on specific tasks.

Social mobile location-based apps like foursquare allow you to reach smartphone users during the 47 percent of the time they spend using their phone for social networking activities. People want to be connected 24-7, and they want personalized, location-based tools and services that are social, reward behavior, and are fun to use. As a local merchant, if you can tap into these reward and gaming platforms, you can reach your customers digitally—wherever they are—and drive them to your physical store.

Marketers are also finding that mobile ads and promotions are more effective than television ads in many cases, because they directly reach targeted users, helping them learn more about products at the point of decision and encouraging those customers to share the offers with friends. John Donahoe, the president of eBay, recently said that mobile is becoming the new way people shop. Although foursquare is not an advertising platform per se, it serves a powerful marketing and advertising role for local merchants who, like Sorge, don't have a large budget for traditional advertising campaigns.

Analysts who follow the mobile category say social networking is the chief factor fueling mobile's growth. These users are sharing information on sites like Twitter or Facebook, playing games (Zynga), or conducting commerce (Groupon). Foursquare straddles each of these three areas, and that's why it's especially powerful. Meeker believes businesses who will win in the growing category will introduce elements of being social, local, gamification (Meeker calls games the ultimate way to engage new audiences), and empowerment. "It's going to be a fascinating decade,"[3] Meeker says. Yes it will be, at least for the winners who choose to participate.

Winners, Laggards, and Losers

Sorge and the other entrepreneurs and business owners featured in this book are clearly social media winners. Their competitors are either laggards or losers. Let me explain the difference between these three categories of business professionals.

Winners

These people are always interested in learning new things. They read books, go to conferences, and are actively engaged in two-way conversations with their employees and customers. Their businesses are notable for exceptional customer service and innovative ideas. They are passionate about driving their business—and industries—forward.

Laggards

These business owners are willing to try new things, but they dip their toes gently into the social media waters. If they feel the slightest chill, they're gone. These are the kind of people who start a Twitter account, post one or two messages, and never do so again. They are the ones who start blogs, lose interest, and stop contributing (95 percent of blogs are ultimately abandoned). They treat foursquare the same way. They may go as far as claiming their venue on foursquare but never offer a special. If they do create a special, they fail to promote it and eventually abandon the initiative if they don't see immediate results.

"We're at the beginning of a new era of social Internet innovators who are reimagining and reinventing a web of people and places."

—**JOHN DOERR,** Partner, Kleiner Perkins

Losers

These folks don't care at all about social media. You're likely to hear them say, "I'm not into that stuff." Their venues are notable for a lack of innovation and poor customer service. They just don't care and rarely last long.

Since the losers don't care, you don't need to worry about them. They won't be outsmarting you anytime soon. The business owners in the first two groups are those who are reading this book. What the laggards need to understand is that with a little effort they can be in the first group—the winners. If not, they risk being outsmarted, outrun, and outdriven.

Social Media Ends Its Dry Spell in the Southwest

Foursquare's early adopters were mostly tech-savvy young adults who lived in large urban areas like New York City and who were on their smartphones all hours of the day. Facebook Places, another geolocation service that lets its users check in and share their location with friends, is validating the activity and making it more acceptable for a broader category of people to check in and check out what's happening in their town. Both Facebook and foursquare are now finding more receptive audiences, including both young and old, tech-savvy and not so technically inclined, people who live in large cities and small cities, and who live in the United States and outside its borders.

I recently gave a keynote presentation at a conference being held on the Mediterranean island of Malta. During lunch with some of the attendees who came from various parts of Europe, someone brought up foursquare. I asked the four or five people at my table if they knew about foursquare, and all of them started nodding, smiling, and sharing stories. We didn't speak the same language, but their enthusiasm told me all that I needed to know.

I knew that foursquare had arrived when I visited the small border town of El Centro, California. I was conducting a workshop for agribusiness leaders, and they decided to hold the seminar in the middle of the desert, about two hours east of San Diego. El Centro isn't exactly known for its bustling restaurant industry. When I got to town, I opened foursquare with no expectations. Much to my surprise, most of the establishments had a mayor and people were checking in. If you think that geolocation apps are just for the big cities, you're wrong. They're heading your way. Will you be a winner or a laggard?

A Sushi Chef Diving into foursquare

The number of Phoenix-area restaurants and venues offering foursquare specials continues to grow as more users join the platform. One restaurant known for its raw food and exotic sea creatures is making an especially big splash. Stingray Sushi is in the heart of Old Town Scottsdale. It's owned by chef and avid Twitter user Andrew Nam. The restaurant is best known for its dishes, elegant ambiance, outdoor patio, and occasional sightings of local sports figures (Shaquille O'Neal was a regular when he played for the Suns). Now it's raising its local profile for its unique foursquare specials that reward diners for repeat visits: "Check in five times and a Sake Bomber or California Roll or Spicy Tuna Roll is on us! Your choice! Spread the word."

Stingray customers are, indeed, spreading the word every day on Twitter and Facebook. Some are simply checking in, and since their foursquare accounts are linked to Twitter, they are automatically broadcasting their whereabouts. But more often than not, these diners are adding a comment to their check-ins, sometimes as short and simple as "yum" or "love some sushi." But many are also touting the special, telling their friends about it, and being incentivized to return.

Business owners around the country could learn a lot from the sushi place in the desert. About twice a month I patronize a sushi restaurant near my office for lunch. It's very good, the fish is fresh, and the prices are reasonable. But with more than 35 restaurant choices on Main Street, I often choose other establishments. If my sushi restaurant offered a foursquare incentive for every fifth check-in, would I visit more often? You bet I would, and each time I checked in or unlocked the special, that information would be shared with my Twitter and Facebook friends.

My local sushi restaurant offers coupons in the newspaper, but since fewer and fewer people are reading the paper, its coupon redemptions do not seem to be having the same impact as they did years ago. Personally, I've never clipped a coupon from the newspaper—for sushi, pizza, or anything else. But I'm on my smartphone every day, I'm using foursquare daily, and I work in downtown Pleasanton right across the street from the restaurant. If the sushi restaurant offered a special like Stingray Sushi does, it would be reaching me directly and I would literally have to walk across the street to enjoy my reward. And just like Main Street in my town, Old Town Scottsdale offers a variety of wonderful dining options. Andrew Nam isn't waiting for another sushi restaurant to outsmart him. He's diving in ahead of them.

Stingray Sushi isn't the only venue in the desert enclave of Scottsdale standing apart from its competitors by engaging an entirely new category of customers. Sweet Republic, an artisan ice cream shop in Scottsdale, uses Twitter to promote its foursquare specials—such as free scoops for the mayor. The Mission, an upscale Latin restaurant, posts instructional videos on its Facebook page and tweets its specials of the day. The foursquare mayor gets a free beer. Other venues that are also using Facebook and Twitter are just beginning to explore the full range of what foursquare has to offer and how it can complement their existing social media efforts. They are learning that a social, location-based service helps them extend the digital conversation to a new group of tech-savvy and mobile consumers who have disposable income (and love to eat).

Most of these Scottsdale restaurants are dabbling in foursquare, offering basic discounts or freebies. But as discussed in previous chapters, there are far more creative uses for foursquare. It's now up to you to take all of the case studies in this book and use the stories to inspire your own creative mobile campaigns. I don't want to leave the impression that every business is on foursquare. They're not. This book is introducing you to the early, creative, and successful adopters. But the vast majority of business owners are still on the sidelines. As more people become comfortable with the concept of checking in on foursquare, Facebook Places, and other platforms, they will be expecting businesses to engage them wherever they are. They will expect better specials. They will expect creative rewards and incentives. Those companies that meet and exceed the expectations of the mobile consumer will win their loyalty. The others will quickly lose relevance.

(143)

Winning Big on a Tiny Budget

Social media has become a priority for local businesses that want to promote and market venues on limited budgets. According to a MerchantCircle survey of small and local businesses across the United States, more than half spend less than $2,500 a year on marketing and most do not intend to raise that budget anytime soon.

Since these local merchants are looking for the most cost-effective ways to reach their customers wherever they are, Facebook is the clear winner (70 percent of respondents use Facebook for marketing). Twitter has also grown in popularity with nearly 40 percent of local merchants using the platform. The survey also found that location-based services like foursquare represent the third leg of the social media equation.

The growth of online and mobile marketing programs is coming at the expense of traditional offline promotions. The business owners who responded to the MerchantCircle survey said they are spending 33 percent less on print advertising than they did a year earlier, 18 percent less on Yellow Pages, and 26 percent less on direct mail. According to Darren Waddell, MerchantCircle's vice president of marketing, "The marketing methods we see gaining the most traction are the ones that offer merchants simplicity, low costs, and immediate results."[4]

The Fast Train to Slow-Roasted Success

Southern California–based Klatch Coffee is one such business shifting its resources online and in the mobile space because that is where their employees and customers are living their lives, sharing information, having conversations, and otherwise engaging with each other and local businesses. Like most areas in the United States, communities that make up the "Inland Empire" east of Los Angeles are dotted with Starbucks coffee shops. How can a small specialty coffee roaster with three stores expect to compete? Since 1993 this small chain has been competing and doing quite well, winning awards and recognition in the process. Klatch Coffee is now famous for its award-winning coffee, outstanding customer service, and an aggressive social media strategy that includes the trifecta of Twitter, Facebook, and foursquare.

Klatch Coffee owner Mike Perry told me that the Klatch Coffee story helps it compete against the larger chains. The story includes cultivating long-term relationships and trading directly with farmers in third-world countries, carefully roasting the beans to bring out the coffee's deepest flavors, and creating a casual and social place for people to meet and to have great conversations. Perry told me that his three stores cater to an affluent clientele who appreciates quality and conversation. Those conversations extend beyond the walls of the coffee shops and on to digital platforms.

Perry's social media efforts include a blog on the company's website that tells the stories of its customers and farmers, and includes videos of barista champions teaching how to make the best espresso (the coffee shop's barista trainer is a two-time national champion). Klatch Coffee also maintains active Twitter and Facebook pages. Once Perry realized his customers were sharing his story with their friends on foursquare, he found a unique tool to extend the conversation to people who were on their smartphones all day long and as an added bonus happened to be his employees and best customers.

If you visit Klatch Coffee in places like Ontario or Rancho Cucamonga, you'll have to visit more than once to unlock a special. Check in five times, and get your coffee drink half off. The special itself isn't newsworthy, but training is. A typical barista at most coffee shops receives about three hours of training. Klatch Coffee trainings can last for three days as baristas learn the art of making lattes. They also learn the art of customer service. The employees know about foursquare, they use it themselves, and when they have a drink ready for the mayor, they serve the drink with a shout-out such as "Double cap on the bar for the mayor!" Perry might not be "knocking out" the Starbucks competition, but while other coffee shops are on the ropes, Perry is going the distance and scoring points with his customers.

Earning the Mobile Consumer's Loyalty

For most businesses, customer loyalty is the key to surviving a recession and thriving in an upturn. The restaurant business is especially sensitive to economic cycles. In one survey, 75 percent of restaurant owners said that loyalty programs helped grow their business in a downturn, and a full 90 percent said their loyalty programs gave them a competitive advantage. "Repeat customers are a very important demographic for restaurant operators to grow their business, and loyalty programs can provide strong incentive to increase visits from those individuals,"[5] according to Hudson Riehle, senior vice president of research for the National Restaurant

Association. "The new research clearly shows the value of operating guest loyalty programs."

Some experts believe that foursquare and Facebook Places will replace the printed loyalty card. As more customers use their mobile phones to receive discounts, promotions, and marketing messages, there is less of a reason for businesses to print loyalty cards. According to experts, there are several reasons why location-based apps are a better option than printed cards for local merchants who want to reward their loyal customers.

1. **You can reach your customers wherever they are and whenever you want.** Local merchants can send messages directly to their customers via e-mail, Twitter, Facebook, or instant messages. With foursquare, you can reach your customers as they are using their phones and entice them with promotions that encourage them to visit your venue when you need them the most. For example, a restaurant could offer a Monday night foursquare special to get people in the door and change the special for the rest of the week.

2. **Your customers are always on their phones.** They're not always carrying their loyalty cards. I've forgotten loyalty cards at home. I never forget my mobile phone.

3. **Promotional startup costs are near zero because there is no need to print cards.** Most loyalty programs require the business owner to print thousands of plastic cards. That means high start-up costs. It can cost $500 to $5,000 to start a card-based loyalty program. Your customers own their phones, and foursquare specials are free.

4. **Using location-based apps eliminates costly POS systems.** Traditional card-based programs are usually tied to a point-of-sale system (POS) installed in each store. These systems cost thousands to buy and maintain. Foursquare has an online dashboard to provide unprecedented and detailed information on who your customers are, when they come in, and so on. Again, the dashboard is free, and it gives small business owners access to information that was very difficult to compile in the past.

5. **Location apps integrate tightly with other social media tools.** Few card-based programs are tied to social media networks. With foursquare, especially when users choose to connect it with Facebook and Twitter, each check-in or reward redemption is shared with hundreds and in many cases thousands of others in an instant. These mobile networking tools help your business expand its social media presence and attract new customers to your business.

Small business owners in the physical world outsmart their competitors by leveraging this new technology to connect with their customers as they explore the world around them with foursquare. Social media is "social," it's personal, and it's shifting to the mobile platform. If you're already using social media tools to reach your customers, social mobile marketing is simply a new and exciting extension of your current efforts. Foursquare's vision is that someday you will visit a new city, and your phone will "wake up" and tell you what to see and what to do. It's not quite there yet, but with features like "Explore," which recommends places to go based on your check-ins, your friends' check-ins, and tips, it's getting much, much closer.

Even More Reasons to Engage Your Mobile Customers

Why should you take foursquare and mobile marketing seriously? A site called B-to-C Marketing asked that very question and came up with the following reasons:

1. **Search engine optimization.** Search engines like Google and Bing will discover your brand on location-based sites and rank your brand more highly because of its legitimacy. Merchants should consider such services as part of their overall search engine optimization (SEO) strategy. In other words, it'll make it easier for you to be found!

147

2. **Smartphone revolution.** The site points out that smartphone growth is nothing less than astounding and that smartphones are poised to overtake the personal computer as the number one way people access the Internet and social media tools. It's estimated that mobile phones will overtake PCs for Web surfing by 2013.

3. **Equally impressive growth of mobile location services.** Among the key factors the site highlights: foursquare grew by 3,400 percent in one year, gets more than two million daily check-ins, and attracts 35,000 new users a day. Merchants need to realize foursquare users are a highly desirable demographic, too. Of the users who check in, 86 percent are younger than age 43, 70 percent have a college degree or higher, and the average income stands at $105,000 (these stats will surely change as the platform becomes more common among users in different age groups). The typical user checks in three to four times a day and likes to share his or her experiences and make recommendations. Geolocation users are 38 percent more likely than the average online adult to say that friends and family ask their opinions before making a purchasing decision. Shouldn't you be reaching these influencers?

4. **Geolocation or geosocial media pushing content to other social networks.** When a user checks in on foursquare, that check-in is often featured on their personal Facebook wall or Twitter stream. The more friends a person has, the more people a brand will be exposed to. Considering that Facebook has 500 million users and Twitter has 200 million, it's a platform that local merchants and brands simply cannot ignore.

5. **Economic benefits.** If you're selling something, you can offer discounts or promotions directly. The site's writers point out, "Even if there is no direct discount, the check-in is the social media equivalent of a word-of-mouth referral."[6] The possibilities of promoting your brand are "endless."

The B-to-C Marketing site concludes, "You have no reason to ignore geosocial media. Geosocial is here to stay, and it can help your inbound marketing results." You're going to see more articles like these in the media. The traditional media has followed a predictable pattern of coverage on the topic of foursquare and geolocation services. First it asked, "What is foursquare?" Then it asked, "Why would anyone want to check in?" Today the media has stopped asking and has started proclaiming, "It's time to get on board." At some point your competitors will be on foursquare. Be there first.

Harvard Discovers foursquare's "Special Dimension"

In February 2011, foursquare was the focus of a Harvard Business School case study. Students were asked why foursquare succeeded while so many other digital media companies have failed. The students concluded that the "context" around a venture matters significantly. In other words, the explosion of smartphones, apps, and other social networking tools is helping foursquare succeed. The students also found that the foursquare team is applying "best practices":

149

- ◆ **Product-obsessed founders.**[7] Cofounders Dennis Crowley and Naveen Selvadurai were consumed with creating the best customer experience. They use it themselves and interact directly with users on Twitter, blogs, and other social media platforms (I include an in-depth conversation with both cofounders at the end of this book).
- ◆ **Hunch driven.** Deep domain knowledge. They didn't need outside knowledge or market research to guide their priorities.
- ◆ **Minimum viable product.** They didn't wait years to perfect the product. They got it out there and solicited user feedback to improve the experience. As a result of the feedback, foursquare continues to roll out new and valuable tools for users and merchants.

What Is Driving foursquare's Rapid Adoption?

The Harvard business students were also asked, "What is driving foursquare's rapid adoption when so many other consumer Internet companies are failing?" The students came up with five reasons:

1. **Game mechanics.** The service is playful, entertaining, and addicting.
2. **NYC launch.** The service had an advantage by starting in a "perfect venue" like New York City, which gave it access to a highly concentrated, social community.
3. **VC Validation.** Having Fred Wilson (cofounder, Union Square Ventures), Ben Horowitz, and others invest in and promote the company gives it great credibility with an inside crowd and "strong tailwinds" (Ben's partner at Andreesen Horowitz, Marc Andreesen, invented the first widely used Web browser and cofounded Netscape).
4. **Win-win for all constituents.** Local merchants make the service. Merchants are incented to promote, discuss, and reward consumers. This creates a "positive feedback loop that transcends the power of a consumer-only service."
5. **Online-offline combination.** The students concluded that foursquare's ability to drive consumers to actually walk into local venues gives it a special dimension worth considering.

Stop Sketching and Start Building

Dennis Crowley once told an interviewer that he doesn't pay close attention to the glowing media accolades he receives because he is passionately focused on pursuing his vision: to build a technology that will wake up your phone and bring it alive. Crowley believes that soon you'll be able to visit a new city and your phone will customize an experience for you, suggesting what to see and what to do. It's not satisfying just to build something, Crowley said. Instead, he says, it's satisfying to be among the first to do it. Entrepreneurs like Crowley find satisfaction in being first. Crowley's advice for entrepreneurs: "Forget about where you want to be and start building. Things happen because you make them happen. Stop sketching and start building."[8]

CHECKING IN

Foursquare cofounder Dennis Crowley says he is continuously surprised at how businesses are using the technology in creative and unique ways. Crowley nailed the reason for foursquare's broad appeal when he answered the question, "Why don't you move the company to San Francisco?" According to Crowley, "The product is better because it's in New York. San Francisco is a big tech hub and has the feel of early adopters. The folks out here don't all work in technology. Our early group of foursquare beta testers were people in the media. They were authors and musicians and people in fashion and finance. I think they gave us more feedback and more ideas than we would have received otherwise."[9]

151

As a local merchant you have the opportunity to be among the first movers in this space. Don't wait for others to pave the way. Don't spend months pouring over Excel spreadsheets and trying to figure out the return on investment (ROI) of engaging your customers on mobile platforms. The social, mobile location space is still very, very young. Most of your competitors are still figuring out what they should be doing on Facebook and Twitter. Your competitors might not be checking in for a while. But they will check in eventually. In March 2011, less than 15 percent of merchants reported doing any sort of mobile marketing. Why? They didn't understand it. Seventy-five percent of merchants said they didn't have a good idea of how to reach consumers via mobile marketing.[10]

You must lead the way. You must be forward thinking and receptive to a changing world. Emerging social networks favor first movers. If you're going to commit, go all in, and do it sooner rather than later. It could be the edge you need to attract new and loyal customers. Stop sketching and start building.

UNLOCK THE POWER

* **Find inspiration in success.** Visit the foursquare pages of the venues featured in this book. Go to their Facebook and Twitter pages as well to see how these brands, businesses, and local merchants coordinate their social media campaigns across the three platforms. You can find more tips on my foursquare brand page (http://foursquare.com/carminegallo).

* **Monitor and engage.** Use a platform like TweetDeck to create search categories for terms such as *foursquare*. By monitoring the check-ins and the conversations people are having on foursquare literally every second of every day, you will be more inspired and emboldened to create campaigns. Also engage your customers directly. Once you begin offering foursquare specials, have conversations with your customers. Commit to spending 10 to 20 minutes a day checking your foursquare dashboard and having conversations with your foursquare customers. Tweet about your specials and promote your specials on your other social networks, too.

* **Hire or identify a social networking spokesperson.** Some of the business owners featured in the book spend hours a day on social media because they realize the power of social media to build their brands. I realize it's not a time commitment you might be ready to make. Then hire someone, even part time, to maintain these conversations and engage your customers in virtual conversations. Once you hire or designate the right person to have social conversations, don't use that person as an excuse to take a hands-off approach to social media. Your customers want to hear directly from you—the business owner or brand manager.

CHAPTER 10

Swarm Masters

> *Adding foursquare to our social media mix shows that we're early adopters and on the cutting edge. That's very important to us as a brand.*
>
> —**MATTHEW RODBARD,** Social Media Manager, Metromix

How to unlock the Swarm badge
Check in to a location where
50 others are also checked in.

Competition is fierce in almost every category of business, but it is especially so in entertainment, and travel and tourism. Businesses in both of these areas are subject to the vagaries of the economy. Any economic shock—stocks, gas, layoffs—can leave these venues reeling. Both brands in this chapter survived and thrived despite challenging economic times and have started to incorporate mobile location-based networking into their marketing mix.

That's Entertainment!

⚲ METROMIX
Anywhere There's a Party, U.S.A.

Metromix bills itself as an ever-expanding, always-obsessive guide to local entertainment. It's hard to argue with that tagline. The guide is available for more than 60 cities across the United States, offering readers tips on where to go and what to do at the hottest restaurants and bars, as well as the latest in music, movies, and entertainment.

Metromix social media manager Matt Rodbard first learned about location-based services when Dennis Crowley had created Dodgeball, an early version of foursquare that he sold to Google, which later discontinued the service. The concept behind Dodgeball was simply to connect friends around New York. Anyone could track their pals to find out where the party was being held. Foursquare, of course, took the concept much further and added the gaming component, which attracted Rodbard. "In the early days people were competing to accrue the most points, not just mayorships. I was trying to become the points leader. But then it evolved. The more friends I acquired, the more powerful the platform became for me as a user."[1]

The foursquare bug had bitten Rodbard. He saw the overlap between foursquare and Metromix, which is essentially a source of the best venues for different categories (16,000 listings in New York alone). Metromix is careful with its marketing budget and was searching for a cost-effective platform to reach users who were increasingly mobile. It was also trying to stand apart from the thousands of outlets people had to choose from when looking for entertainment—newspapers, magazines, blogs, Twitter, Facebook, and so on.

Foursquare offered Metromix a unique feature the others did not—the ability to push recommendations to its followers as they neared venues. Metromix editorial staffers continuously add tips for hundreds of their favorite local spots. Looking for the best yakitori joint on St. Marks? Wicker Park's famous $5 tamale guy? The strongest margarita in town? Metromix has your back.

"It has benefited us as a brand because once people start following the Metromix brand page (18,000 followers and growing), our brand is push-notified into their world. We may have created a tip for the actual location or a nearby location. A user might be checking in to a bar without knowing about the great tapas restaurant next door. Even if they don't go to the restaurant, they recognize Metromix as a sophisticated entertainment guide on the cutting edge," says Rodbard.

Impressions are the name of the game for a site like Metromix—eyeballs. The more people who visit the Metromix family websites, the more the company can charge for advertising and partnerships. "We're in the business of page views," says Rodbard. "Building our readership through foursquare is absolutely invaluable."

CHECKING IN

"Outsmart the competition by making your mayor a spokesperson for your venue. Give that person a weekly allotment of coupons, discounts, or drink tickets that he or she can share with others. Giving the mayor a free drink is cool, but it affects only one person. Empower the mayor to share your venue with friends."

—MATT RODBARD,
Social Media Manager, Metromix

Metromix outsmarts its competitors by embracing foursquare and thinking differently about how to use the platform. For example, Metromix does not own its venues and does not offer specials. But they can engage mayors. Metromix provides original articles in a series called Foursquare File. Editors will find the mayor of an establishment, contact him or her on Twitter, and ask for an interview. They have the article coincide with a planned theme like "best barbeque," and so on. In one article, Metromix interviewed two people battling it out for mayor of a New York City SoHo joint called Delicatessen. The rivalry got so intense the restaurant created a cocktail for both competitors and hosted a victory party for the winner. Rodbard says the articles are wildly popular and are often shared on Twitter, extending the Metromix brand even further, far more than their marketing budget would have allowed.

Although you may have yet to visit the "101 newest NYC restaurants" or the "top 30 shows in Chicago" or even the "best 25 clubs in Miami," if you're ever near one of these venues, you might see a Metromix branded tip on your foursquare app. By making it easier to explore restaurants, bars, clubs, and events in your city, Metromix has discovered a way to outsmart its competition and have a good time doing it!

What Happens in Vegas Gets Shared Outside Vegas

WYNN HOTELS
Las Vegas, Nevada

The stunning hotel, rooms, restaurants, shows, and golf course at Wynn Las Vegas and its sister hotel, Encore, make the Wynn one of the most elegant resorts in the world. Despite its world-class elegance, it's not always easy to fill the Wynn's 5,000 rooms and 18 restaurants, especially when there's a downturn in the economy.

Owner Steve Wynn is a master of customer service, so it wasn't a surprise to see the Wynn hotels add foursquare specials for their increasingly mobile-savvy guests. Foursquare gives the hotel the ability to instantly change the specials as the shows change. One special read:

Check-In Special. Show this check-in at the box office and receive $15 off *Sinatra Dance with Me* tickets. Offer valid on all ticket prices and shows. (The Sinatra show combined Frank Sinatra music, big band music, and professional dancers. By the time you read this, the Wynn special might have changed based on a new show the Wynn needs to promote.)

Wynn knows that people who have a bad hotel experience are much more likely to talk about it than those who have a good experience. But foursquare is much more of a community, and instead of getting nothing but complaints, a hotel like the Wynn receives tips from guests on everything from which rooms have the best views to restaurant recommendations and much, much more (a venue can encourage positive discussion by offering a special or reward for guests who add a tip). While many people will leave tips such as "awesome hotel" or "the buffet here is amazing," more often than not the tips offer specific, detailed, and insightful information that help other guests make their stays more enjoyable. Here are some examples of tips left at Wynn's Encore hotel:

- **Vegas Chatter.** Rooms are great, but to avoid the nightclub music from Surrender, request a room on opposite side of building. (This is a good tip if I need some quiet. But it also reminds me that the rooms are wonderful, and it tells me there's a hot nightclub around the corner.)
- **Tim M.** Caught the Dueling Pianos show in the Eastside Lounge. It was great. Perfect finish to the night after a wonderful meal at the Botero. (This tip offers a recommendation for a steak dinner and music to end the night.)
- **Maya B.** Always ask upon check-in if they have any suites available. You can usually upgrade for $50 or more a night. (Great tip that you don't see on the hotel website.)

(158) In less than one year on foursquare, the Wynn hotels had registered nearly 20,000 check-ins. Keep in mind that during much of that year foursquare was growing its user base and had nowhere near the number of users it has today.

CHECKING IN

The Wynn hotel's marketing staff have also seeded the foursquare page with their own tips that call attention to unique features in the hotel. For example, a foursquare user might learn that the red chandeliers in Encore were inspired by the twirling of a woman's skirt and are made from Murano glass. The staff are actively involved in reaching out to foursquare users and will continue to use foursquare's exclusive merchant dashboard and its statistics to learn more about their guests.

Most visitors to Las Vegas already have their hotels booked by the time they arrive. So while Wynn might not be "outsmarting" the other hotels by enticing guests through the doors at the point of their decision, the Wynn's foursquare strategy is intended to complement and improve its luxury service. The Wynn caters to people with refined tastes who are also smartphone users. By partnering with foursquare the hotel offers a Wynn-Win for the brand and its guests.

UNLOCK THE POWER

+ **Include your staff.** Wynn staff are encouraged to create content for foursquare and other social media platforms. Include the contributions of a broader team so you're not doing all the social media outreach yourself!
+ **Offer tips outside the beaten path.** Be creative with your content. Offer insights and tips your customers will not find anywhere else.

CHAPTER 11

Incentivize Your Customers

Today the most interesting business models are finding ways to make money around Free.

—CHRIS ANDERSON, Author, Editor-in-Chief, *Wired*

Sassy Thomas suffers from severe chronic fatigue syndrome (CFS). She rarely leaves her house in the small village of Thrapston, Northamptonshire, in the United Kingdom. Thomas's illness is so debilitating that she needs help with her personal care and to step out of the house. Thomas told me in an e-mail exchange, "Because of my fatigue and the pain I feel, it's an ordeal to get out of the house. By the time I'm dressed, I'm exhausted and have lost all motivation to go anywhere."[1] Foursquare has changed her life "massively." Whether you own a small business or manage a global brand, you'll want to hear about Thomas's remarkable story because it offers valuable lessons for businesses seeking to engage customers on a deeper level.

One Small Step for foursquare, One Giant Leap for Thomas

Thomas learned about foursquare from a Facebook friend and decided to join. She thought the idea of checking in to places around town and sharing her check-ins with friends on her social networks would motivate her in some small way. For people suffering from CFS, the exhaustion they experience is debilitating. Thomas was looking for anything that would force her to take a few steps out the door. Since foursquare's mission is to help people explore their world by turning life into a game, Thomas considered foursquare an incentive that might provide the keys to her recovery.

A Badge Weekend Brought Her Back

Thomas and her boyfriend planned a foursquare "badge weekend." Her boyfriend excitedly assisted with the planning and rented a wheelchair so Thomas could check in to as many venues as possible.

The designated Saturday came along, and Thomas was ready with her list of venues that she had researched online—venues that were reasonably close and offered the best opportunities to unlock badges. "It was a beautiful summer day, and it turned out to be the best day I had had in months," says Thomas.

The day started with a boat trip so Thomas could earn the I'm on a Boat badge, earned for checking in to any venue tagged "boat." On another stop, Thomas discovered a small pub nearby where she had one of the best meals of her life. Thomas and her boyfriend then headed to a nearby town to drop into a Starbucks (the closest one to her rural village). "I'm not a coffee drinker at all, so it was all new to me," says Thomas. "I had the most gorgeous hazelnut hot chocolate and a big slice of cake!" Later in the day they went to a movie theater and checked in so Thomas could earn credits toward the Zoetrope badge (unlocked with 10 check-ins to movie theaters). "The cinema is usually a nightmare for me because of the travel," says Thomas.

After the movie, Thomas and her boyfriend went to a new pizza place to earn points toward the Pizzaiola badge. Although neither of them had been to the pizzeria before, the restaurant has since become their favorite pizza place. "For me it was an amazing achievement to accomplish so much and to enjoy it. My joy lasted for weeks and kept the 'cabin fever' at bay. I still look back on that day and smile," says Thomas.

The definition of *incentive* is something that incites or tends to incite to action or greater effort—a reward for increased productivity. On that foursquare weekend, Thomas was incentivized to put in greater effort to leave the house and to be more productive. A similar psychological incentive motivates thousands of foursquare users to hit the gym more frequently to earn the Gym Rat badge, unlocked with 10 visits to a gym in 30 days. Foursquare's founders are big believers in the power of software to encourage and motivate behavior. For Thomas, the ability to share her achievements with friends on

163

foursquare, Twitter, and Facebook provided an even greater psychological reward for checking in and earning badges. Sharing her check-ins provided another type of social incentive for Thomas because her friends would congratulate her, ask about her experiences, and offer words of encouragement.

From Super Tired to Superuser

Thomas loved foursquare so much she became a superuser. This status is not to be confused with the Super User badge. Foursquare superusers are users who are very active with foursquare and who are handpicked by the foursquare staff to edit venues, merge duplicate venues, close fake venues, and ultimately keep the database nice and clean. "One thing I miss is being able to do things for others instead of having them do things for me all the time. Being a superuser makes me feel good about myself even though I'm stuck indoors, because I can help people all over the world. I also learn about cool places from seeing my friends' check-ins!"

Once business owners understand the powerful built-in incentives that foursquare provides, they can leverage the platform to encourage repeat visits or to induce people to choose their establishment over the competition.

Foursquare motivated Thomas to leave the house and explore her neighborhood. But badges and specials offer Thomas incentives to return to her newly discovered venues again and again. If foursquare can incentivize a woman who had been housebound for two weeks to visit establishments in her tiny English village, imagine what it could do for your business.

Reaching Your Customers Wherever They Are

When a user opens foursquare on her smartphone, she sees a list of places in her immediate vicinity along with a list of specials in the vicinity. Foursquare is accessing the user's GPS receiver to pinpoint her location and to list nearby locations.

The algorithm is created in such a way as to give every user a unique experience. Your experience will be slightly different than it is for another user down the block and vastly different than it is for a user across town. Foursquare's Explore feature will return results based on the history of your check-ins and the behavior of your friends. Again, the experience is customized for the individual. The radius that foursquare covers is dynamic. The foursquare app will show the 30 closest places or as many as will fill up the screen. If a user is in the middle of a Nebraska cornfield, the "closest" 30 venues might fall within a radius of two miles or more. In New York, the screen might be filled with venues in a radius of two square blocks.

Now here's where it really gets interesting for businesses. Once a business owner or manager visits the foursquare website, finds his establishment, and claims the venue, he can create up to seven types of specials to attract new customers or reward existing customers. A foursquare user exploring her city simply clicks the bright orange "Special Here" banner to get more information about the reward, discount, or promotion the manager created. That means if users check in to your venue, they will see the special. But if they are near your establishment *or in a competitor's venue*, they will see a Special Nearby banner pointing them right to your business. It's like walking right up to customers in another store and handing them a coupon for your business—a coupon they can redeem immediately simply by showing the cashier their phone. This is a powerful way of enticing people to try your place over your competitors or simply introducing your brand to a new customer.

A Delicious and Hearty Special

On a trip to La Jolla, California, I stayed in a hotel that I had never tried before—Hyatt Regency Grand. On the sprawling property there were four restaurants vying for my attention. Since I arrived at noon, I decided to have lunch, but where? The hotel and the restaurants were completely new to me. I opened foursquare and checked in to the hotel. I noticed a

Special Nearby banner. I clicked the tab and the banner, and it took me to a special at Michael's restaurant that read:

> Show this to a bartender & enjoy a complimentary cheese or chicken quesadilla at Michael's Lounge, our lobby bar. Follow Michael's on Facebook.com for other special offers.

I looked up from my phone and sure enough, I was standing right outside the restaurant. I walked into the bar, sat down, showed my phone to the gregarious bartender who knew all about the special, and enjoyed a delicious (and hearty) quesadilla 10 minutes later. I also ordered an expensive glass of wine and gave the bartender a nice tip. The bartender told me that customers come in every day to unlock the promotion (only available on first-time check-ins). When I asked the bartender if he gets any benefit from giving away free food, he said, "Nobody comes in for just the free quesadilla and leaves. They usually buy drinks for themselves and their friends, or order more appetizers or entrées." Everybody wins with this type of special—the restaurant, the bartender, and me, the hungry customer.

Michael's at the Hyatt Regency outsmarted the competition that day by being the only one to offer a special that anyone with a smartphone could redeem—an incentive for me to try the restaurant over others nearby. Now if I had an insatiable desire for sushi on that given afternoon, no special at Michael's—quesadilla or otherwise—would have prevented

CHECKING IN

Competition, especially in the restaurant industry, is fierce. Your customers are easily wooed. Foursquare specials give your customers a reason—and incentive—to enter your establishment instead of another. Claim your venue and begin offering specials immediately. It takes about five minutes or less to create a special, and best of all, it's free.

me from walking across the street to the upscale sushi restaurant I had spotted as I entered the hotel. A special doesn't guarantee a sale, but it offers a compelling incentive that reaches your potential customers at the moment of their purchase decision.

A New Cup of Special Brewing at Starbucks

Starbucks marked its 40th anniversary on Friday, March 12, 2011, and it chose foursquare to help it celebrate. The chain rolled out a new logo and launched in-store events called Tribute Days. Starbucks had opened its doors four decades earlier with one coffee shop in Seattle's Pike Place Market and then grew into one of the most recognizable brands in the world. The original Starbucks at 1912 Pike Place (at Stewart Street) had registered more than 6,200 foursquare check-ins by the Tribute weekend. Starbucks was one of the first national brands to offer a customized badge on foursquare (the Barista badge could be unlocked with a visit to five different locations).

On March 12th, foursquare users who checked in could unlock the limited-edition Starbucks Tribute badge and have the chance to win a $40 gift card. Users who unlocked the badge saw this message:

167

> Thank you. We started in 1971 and are turning 40. You've earned this badge and a chance to win a $40 Starbucks card.

Starbucks' limited-edition badge and the sweepstakes inspired its customers (and perhaps new customers) to take action, giving them an extra incentive to visit the store during the promotion window.

Starbucks and Michael's at the La Jolla Hyatt Regency both took advantage of foursquare's specials in different ways, proving that mobile social marketing can incentivize customers of global brands or single-store establishments. In fact, local merchants and small business owners now have a powerful tool to compete against their more established competitors.

Attracting New Customers in a Flash

Foursquare offers several types of specials through its Merchant Platform. Businesses can even offer multiple specials for different categories of customers. See Figure 11.1. One venue—a Mexican restaurant, for example—might wish to offer the following tiered incentives:

- **Mayor Special:** Free appetizer with entrée. (unlocked for the mayor)
- **Check-in Special:** Free drink upon check-in. (unlocked with every check-in)
- **Newbie Special:** Thanks for checking in. Show screen to any waiter, and get a free dessert on us! (unlocked on first check-in)
- **Loyalty Special:** Free signature cocktail on every third check-in. (unlocked every three check-ins)
- **Special Offer:** Visit us on Super Bowl Sunday, and get a free plate of nachos for your entire table. (unlocked for special conditions)

FIGURE 11.1

Foursquare offers several types of specials through its Merchant Platform.

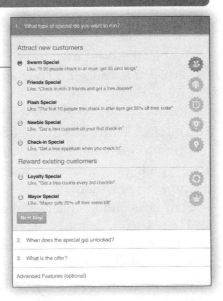

When foursquare first introduced tiered merchant specials in 2011, 10 national brands joined foursquare to launch the new platform. Their introductory specials offered several creative examples of what other businesses could do with the new tools. Keep in mind these are just examples of the type of specials a brand or local merchant can create. Since businesses can—and should—change their specials frequently, these specials are just a snapshot of what has been created.

Flash Specials

These mirror the type of "door buster" deals businesses offer on Black Friday. But with these new mobile marketing promotions, any business can turn any day into Black Friday.

- **Sports Authority:** The first to check in at each store after 11:00 A.M. scored a free gift card for $20.
- **Barnes & Noble:** The first 10 people to check in after 10:00 A.M. received $10 off a NOOK color e-reader.
- **Toys"R"Us:** The first 5 people to check in after 11:00 A.M. at the Toys"R"Us at the Times Square location in New York City got their photos displayed on a giant marquee on Times Square.

Friends Specials

A lot of people go out with their friends, so foursquare provides a way for businesses to reward customers and their friends who check in together (see Figure 11.2).

- **H&M Clothing:** Anyone who checked in along with three friends would get 24 percent off any item. Everyone got to unlock the special.
- **Whole Foods Market:** Anyone who checked in with a friend at any participating location between 11:00 A.M. and 4:00 P.M. received a free cookie.
- **Chili's Grill & Bar:** Anyone who checked in with three or more friends received a free appetizer for the whole table.

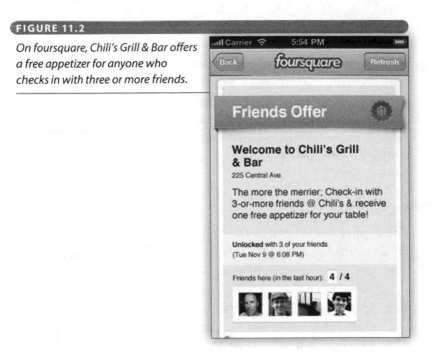

FIGURE 11.2

On foursquare, Chili's Grill & Bar offers a free appetizer for anyone who checks in with three or more friends.

Swarm Offer

Swarms are very popular on foursquare as users like to unlock the Swarm badge for being in the same venue with a large number of other users. (A Swarm badge is unlocked when a user is checked in the same venue along with 50 other foursquare check-ins. The Super Duper Swarm badge is unlocked when 500 people check in, and the Epic Swarm badge is unlocked when 1,000 or more are checked in.) A business, however, does not need to attract that many people to offer a Swarm special. It's up to the business to decide how many people constitute a swarm to unlock the special.

- **Applebee's:** Free mozzarella sticks if five people checked in after 9:00 P.M. The appetizers were given to anyone who showed their phone with the unlocked special.

Newbie Special

With this special, any business can entice new customers to give them a try.

- **Coffee Bean & Tea Leaf:** First-time check-ins were given $1 off any drink.
- **Arby's:** First-time check-ins received $1 off Arby's new Angus Three Cheese & Bacon burger. Arby's rolled out this special at all of its locations as part of a national campaign to introduce Americans to the new burger.
- **RadioShack:** The electronics chain began offering 20 percent discounts to all customers who checked in for the first time (5,000 locations nationwide participated in the launch).

RadioShack was one of the first national brands to demonstrate the versatility of the new specials. On the day it launched its Newbie special, RadioShack also introduced a Check-In special: "Check in at RadioShack for 10% off qualifying purchases. Check in enough times to earn a spot as the mayor of this store and get 20% off!" Visitors to RadioShack who checked in on foursquare were greeted with both specials at the same time, offering incentives to newbies, mayors, and anyone else who checked in. Let's take an even closer look at RadioShack, the brand, and how it has attracted new and valuable customers thanks to foursquare.

Mobile Marketing Redefines a Brand

If you're like me, then you think about RadioShack as a place to buy parts and pieces—the cables, wires, batteries, and gadgets that make electronic devices work. That common perception of the brand is partly true, but it's not the whole story. Through its 6,000 locations across North America, RadioShack has become one of the leading third-party mobile and wireless retailers in the United States. It carries every leading brand of mobile phone, including iPhone 4, BlackBerry, HTC, EVO 4G, Samsung, and Motorola products. "Our marketing mission is to redefine RadioShack for consumers, to contemporize the brand, and to leverage the conversation around mobility,"[2] says Lee Applbaum, RadioShack's chief marketing officer.

"We want to be known for our leading brands and innovative products."

When Applbaum and his team first began hearing about foursquare, it didn't take them long to see that it was a natural fit with their marketing mission. As a brand that wants to spread the word that it is a leader in mobility, it's also important that its 35,000 store associates be seen as knowledgeable about all things mobile. Add to the mix the fact that RadioShack has an unrivaled network of physical locations and the combination lends itself to a location-based marketing promotion. Enter foursquare, which had the added bonus of offering a game layer that made it "inherently sticky."

Foursquare's demographic is alluring to a brand like RadioShack. Early adopters are by nature young, mobile, and engaged. "Those are the people we need to attract," says Applbaum. "We want them to know that we're innovative as a mobile authority. This is where we want to be."

RadioShack first used foursquare as a critical component of its social media campaign during the 2010 holiday season. The RadioShack theme for the campaign was titled "Holiday Heroes." The idea behind the campaign was that holidays were stressful. If you wanted to be the person who got the perfect gift and a high five, visit RadioShack. The television ads were clever and funny. RadioShack's foursquare promotion was linked to the theme and worked like this: Followers of RadioShack could unlock a customized Holiday Hero badge by checking in to two of three designated holiday hero "hotspots": gyms (a superhero has to stay fit), coffee shops (a superhero needs to recharge), or a place of transit, like an airport or train station (a superhero needs a fast way to reach his or her destination). Once a user had checked in to two places, a check-in at RadioShack unlocked the badge, which could be redeemed for a store discount of 20 percent. Foursquare users who did not participate in the Holiday Hero campaign—and didn't want to bother with the other check-ins—were still offered a 10 percent discount just for checking in to a RadioShack. Mayors were entitled to 15 percent discounts.

The campaign started on November 15th and ended on December 31st. RadioShack communicated its foursquare promotion via complementary social media like Facebook (www.facebook.com/RadioShack) and Twitter (www.twitter.com/RadioShack). RadioShack also advertised its campaign in conventional and digital media with circulars, flyers, and e-mails.

RadioShack's foursquare promotion was a huge success. Applbaum cites the following metrics:

◆ Foursquare users who unlocked the specials or the badge spent more money. "The average spend of the foursquare users during that promotion was three-and-a-half times that of the average RadioShack consumer," according to Applbaum. "That's a big number." Applbaum believes in the concept of "reciprocity." He thinks that if you ask a consumer to check in to unlock a special, especially two or three different times, that consumer is expecting something in return. If they get a 20 percent discount and they went through the steps of checking in, they might as well use the discount for something substantial.

◆ Foursquare users unlocked the specials to buy mobile phones and other higher-ticket items. "This fits into our strategy to enhance awareness for RadioShack in the wireless and mobile space. Foursquare users spent more on categories that are important to our brand and for our business growth."

◆ The promotion was widely covered by major media including the *Wall Street Journal* and influential blogs and sites. "For the investment community and for a brand that wants to be relevant in the mobile conversation, that buzz is great for the brand."

Many businesses join social media platforms for one reason—they want to show their consumers that they're cool. Applbaum sees it differently. "What we have found with Twitter and foursquare is that these are meaningful traffic and sales drivers." RadioShack wasn't the first brand on four-

CHECKING IN

"Define your goals. At RadioShack we can show that foursquare engagements are profitable for us, driving traffic and sales. But there is nothing wrong with the simple goal of showing your customers that you are hip, relevant, innovative, and that you want to be involved in the social conversation. If that's your only goal, it's OK."

—**LEE APPLBAUM,** Chief Marketing Officer, RadioShack

square, but it intends to play a major role as foursquare rolls out new and enhanced merchant tools.

Exploring Their World and Coming Across Yours

A foursquare feature called Explore offers users a way to learn more about a city based on information from their previous check-ins and their friends' check-ins. "We started foursquare with the idea of making cities easier to use,"[3] says foursquare cofounder Dennis Crowley. "We've long wanted to build those things that can augment your experience of the real world—software that introduces you to new places and new experiences." Explore gets foursquare closer to that vision with the introduction of a truly personalized recommendation engine.

The idea behind Explore is pretty simple: tell foursquare what you're looking for and it will help you find something nearby. The suggestions are based on a little of everything:

◆ places you've been
◆ places your friends have visited
◆ your loyalty to your favorite places

- the categories and types of places you visit
- what's popular with other users
- the day of the week
- places with great tips

This is only the beginning. Foursquare crunches millions of data points and gets a little smarter with each additional check-in and tip. That means foursquare will continue to grow as a personalized concierge that travels with you wherever you go.

I used the Explore tab for the first time at the Los Angeles International Airport. The Explore tab allows a user to search for categories of venues such as food, coffee, nightlife, shops, entertainment, or anything else you can think of. It also tells you *why* it suggested those venues.

I selected the tab for "food," and foursquare returned several locations based on criteria such as where I had eaten before, the types of establishments I've frequented, and the area restaurants popular with foursquare users. Foursquare suggested one restaurant because I had been to that chain before (but in a different location). It wanted to tell me that this restaurant chain had a location right around the corner in the airport. The software recommended another restaurant because it was similar in style to other restaurants I had checked in to. Other venues were featured because they were popular with foursquare users.

Places that are attracting more users at the time of your search are given top billing and labeled as "trending." These trends can help provide real-time analytics for local businesses, offering endless possibilities to cross-promote your venue. For example, a pizza parlor might notice that local bars and restaurants are "trending" higher after local college basketball games at the nearby stadium. The restaurant might target those young fans, many of whom are already on their smartphones, by creating a Flash special that starts immediately after the game and ends at midnight.

When a user searches for nearby places on foursquare, the software also displays a banner that brings up all of the specials near your location. A local merchant would want to show up in this list, but of course, if the merchant does not offer an incentive in the form of a special, then it will never be included in this valuable piece of real estate.

The trending feature also rewards merchants who have venues with a lot of tips posted by foursquare users. Savvy merchants quickly realized they could show up in the specials list and earn higher trend rankings by offering one creative special: reward users for leaving tips. When a new store opens in a Westfield mall, for example, some locations reward the first 25 people who leave a tip with a $5 Starbucks gift card (or a gift card from another store in the mall).

A Hot Idea for a Cold Treat

I work in an office on Main Street in downtown Pleasanton, California. Dozens of restaurants, coffee shops, wine bars, and ice cream and candy shops line the street for about seven blocks. During the school year on most weekdays at 3:00 P.M., at least 50 to 100 kids from the two nearby high schools gather in the plaza across the street from my office, directly in front of a popular ice cream parlor.

On a hot day the line is out the door and the tables are filled. The franchise owner says he has no problem bringing in business on warm spring or summer days and relies on those days to make up for slower times during inclement weather or when other events in town are drawing people away from Main Street (the county fairgrounds are less than one mile away). After interviewing dozens of businesses for this book, I believe foursquare and mobile marketing tools could offer this franchise owner a *free* solution to build business every day of the week, rain or shine. You see, those kids are all on their smartphones, they love ice cream, and they are standing right outside the door.

The ice cream parlor scenario is an example of how a creative, forward-thinking franchise owner who just read this book could create unique incentives to attract new and existing customers. Let's assume I'm a new franchise owner who just took over the ice cream store. I have two choices to market and advertise the store: continue doing what the previous owner did or create something entirely new, innovative, and buzzworthy.

The previous owner of the ice cream store bought space in local newspapers and offered coupons that customers could clip and bring in for a $1 discount. How many of those students standing outside the store read the local newspaper, let alone cut out a coupon so they can save a buck? I'll go on a limb here and guess "zero." Now what else can I do to advertise the ice cream store I just took over? I could hire a human directional to wave a sign on the corner. Again, how many students are going to buy ice cream on a cold day because they saw a guy out front waving a sign? Again, I'll guess "zero." I could advertise on local television and blow through my entire year's marketing budget in one television spot. And again, how many students standing outside my store on a cold day are going to enter the ice cream parlor because they remember seeing a television ad that ran two weeks prior? OK, maybe "one." And in exchange for that person spending $2 for an ice cream cone, I spent thousands of dollars for television time. None of these options make sense anymore, especially when free and powerful marketing tools are at my very fingertips.

If I managed this franchise, I would blow away the competition in town and be the talk of the entire franchise community by racing to the Internet, claiming my venue on foursquare, and offering specials that would attract students into my store on hot days, cold days, rainy days, and every day in between. It would take me about 30 minutes to set up my venue and another 5 minutes to create a special. My total marketing cost would be zero, except for the time I spent creating the special and the 20 minutes I'll have to spend training the staff. Table 11.1 lists some sample specials I could offer. Following the table are explanations for why each special would work.

TABLE 11.1

SAMPLE FOURSQUARE SPECIALS FOR ICE CREAM CUSTOMERS

Type of Special	Description of the Special
Mayor	The mayor is always treated like a king (or queen) here. Just come in, show us that you're the mayor, and a free large ice cream with one topping is yours!
Newbie	Check in for the first time, and get one of our new hot creations like lava cake or a hot fudge sundae. It's on us!
Swarm	If 20 people are checked in at once, everyone gets a large ice cream for the price of a small. Tell your friends, and create a swarm!
Loyalty	Get three free toppings with every third check-in.
Flash	It's cold outside, so drop in to stay warm! The first 50 people who check in today after 3 P.M. receive 50 percent off any of our new hot indulgences. Lava cake, anyone?

Why My Ice Cream Specials Would Work

Mayor Special. A free "large" ice cream just for showing your phone? The competition among the kids would be intense. My special would create awareness for my new mobile marketing promotion and ignite a competitive frenzy. A large-size ice cream at this store typically costs the customer $4 and includes one free topping. It's likely that the mayor will buy additional toppings, and the competition it would create would bring in far more business than I would lose by giving someone a large scoop of free ice cream.

Upon launching this mayor's special, I would check to see if my venue already had a mayor. Although these are hypothetical specials that I created for this particular ice cream shop, when I checked I discovered that it really did have a foursquare mayor. She's a young lady who goes by Jamie L. Jamie is an avid foursquare user who checks in frequently and is the mayor of 18 other spots in town. She leaves tips, earns badges, and shares experiences with her friends. Jamie has 55 friends. Judging by the photographs of her friends, they are all young people (late teens to mid-20s) and they all live in the area.

I checked the profiles of each of Jamie's friends and totaled how many friends each had. Together Jamie's 55 friends were connected with 2,000 other friends—nearly all of whom are in her age range and live in town. This tells me that if I create a mayor's special, it would spark a frenzy among Jamie's friends. I can even reach out directly to Jamie on Twitter and congratulate her for being the mayor and invite her in to create her own special, an experience she will certainly share with her friends (and their friends). With one simple—and free—promotion, my ice cream shop would instantly become the talk of the town.

Newbie Special. This ice cream parlor recently began offering "hot" treats like lava cakes and hot fudge sundaes. This Newbie special would serve two purposes—getting customers comfortable with checking in and introducing them to the new menu choices.

Swarm Special. The kids (and parents) outside the store all know that a large is a sizable amount of delicious ice cream and is the most expensive cup. This Swarm special would have everyone talking and joining forces to unlock the special. The kids who are not familiar with foursquare could download the app in 30 seconds and be ready to participate.

Loyalty Special. Frequency-based loyalty specials are very successful at enticing customers to return. The toppings at this ice cream parlor can easily turn a $2 scoop into a $6 indulgence. In downtown Pleasanton, there are two soft-serve yogurt stores and another ice cream shop. I visit all of them since I love ice cream and yogurt. But if this particular store offered three free toppings with every third check-in, I would have a strong incentive to visit it over the others.

Flash Special. This is the equivalent of a door buster. Very few people walk into ice cream shops when it's cold outside, but very few people also know about this ice cream parlor's new "hot" menu choices. This Flash special would introduce my customers to the new menu and attract a line that might go out the door. It would also introduce my customers to the fact that I'm on foursquare, and they would see my other specials as well. There's no downside to this special. It's free to set up. Yes, I'm offering a deep discount, but let's assume I would expect to sell only 5 hot creations on a cold day—and I end up selling 50 or more due to my foursquare special. Even at a discount I come out way ahead.

Using foursquare's merchant tools, this ice cream parlor could be very creative with its incentives and offer tiered specials a well. It also helps the ice cream shop tell its story. Think about it. Clipping a coupon to save a buck on ice cream doesn't establish an emotional connection with the brand. By rewarding the mayor in a fun, creative way, encouraging students to leave a tip, or introducing new "hot" menu items on a cold day, the store is creating a far deeper and more engaging relationship with its customers.

As the new (hypothetical) franchise owner of this ice cream parlor, I also need to realize that poor training can turn my new promotion into a bust. If a customer unlocks a special and shows it to a clueless employee, that customer may not return, and even worse, may share the bad experience with her mobile friends. I happen to know that the existing franchise owner trains new employees (typically high school and college-age kids) every season. Since he has to train them anyway, taking another 15 to 20 minutes to teach them about the foursquare specials is no big deal. He should explain foursquare and show them what the specials look like on a smartphone. If I were training the employees, I would go one step further and get them to advertise our new mobile promotions. A conversation between an employee and the customer might go something like this:

Employee: Do you know about our foursquare special?
Customer: No, what's foursquare?
Employee: It's a free social networking app. Just download it to your smartphone, check in to this ice cream parlor, and redeem our amazing specials. We're running a Newbie

special. Get a free medium ice cream and one topping for your first check-in. It'll only take you a few seconds to download the app and redeem the special. You can do it right now if you'd like.

Most businesses have very, very poor customer service and terribly inadequate staff training. If you offer a frequency-based incentive such as "check in three times and get a free large for the price of a small," you're just inviting patrons to experience your poor service three times. If that's the case, don't spend your time wondering why your foursquare campaign is failing to gain traction. It's not foursquare. It's you. And if you're not prepared to improve the overall customer service experience in your establishment, then no type of social media—mobile or otherwise—will help you.

Based on my experience with the businesses featured in this book, I know these specials would work as powerful incentives for this ice cream parlor. Why isn't the franchise owner doing this? Because he doesn't know about it, and even

181

CHECKING IN

Make it easy for your employees to enter the special in your point-of-sale system. You can do so simply by adding a code in the text of the special. The message is not for customers; it's for your employees. For example, Zales, a specialty diamond retailer with 1,870 stores in the United States and Canada, offered this special: "Check in and unlock $50 off your $300 purchase." It added one sentence: "Associates enter code 104SQR000000018 at checkout." Zales trains its staff, but with thousands of employees across the continent, it didn't want to take a chance that its foursquare promotion would backfire because some of its employees didn't know about it. One sentence resolves a lot of potential problems.

if he has heard about foursquare, he might not understand how powerful it could be for his business. He'll know now.

He Who Offers the Best Special Wins

Some of the best deals offer foursquare users strong incentives to check in again and again. If my hypothetical ice cream shop

TABLE 11.2

COFFEE/TEA VENUE SPECIAL EXAMPLES

Coffee/Tea Venue	Special (Incentive)	Mayor Special
Café Coffee Day (Bangalore, India's largest chain of coffee shops)	Check in three times and get a 15 percent discount on your third check-in.	Mayor gets free coffee every day and 20 percent discount.
Epoch Coffee Bar & Desserterie (Hong Kong chain of coffee shops)	Check in, buy a coffee, and get a free "financier," a specialty dessert.	
Goswell Road Coffee (Greater London)		The *Financial Times* rewarded students who frequent this coffee shop with a free *Financial Times* subscription for the mayor.
Om Shan Tea (San Francisco)	A tea room that gives foursquare users 10 percent off their teas if they bring in sewing or knitting on Sundays and check in.	
Progress Coffee (Austin, Texas)	Friends special. From 7 to 9:30 A.M., buy a breakfast biscuit and get a second biscuit free for your friend.	The mayor gets a drink named after him or her and gets it free when he or she comes in.

ideas aren't enough to fuel your creativity, Tables 11.2 through 11.5 list more examples from venues around the world that might give you a jump start. These deals might have changed by the time you read this. I hope they have. Specials need to rotate and be kept fresh to offer the best incentives, encourage repeat business, and to battle check-in fatigue!

TABLE 11.3

NON-RESTAURANT VENUE SPECIAL EXAMPLES

Venue	Special (Incentive)	Mayor Special
Arcane Properties (Southern California Real Estate firm)	Rewards foursquare users with $1,000 cash if they check in, notify the firm about a property someone is trying to sell, and the firm decides to buy the property.	
Elite Photography Studio (Hong Kong)	Newbie special. First-time check-in receives 40 percent discount on portrait session and includes five fully edited photos of your choice.	
Hollywood & Highland Center (also known as H&H; Los Angeles shopping mall)	Shopping center that incentivizes spending behavior in return for two free movie passes. A user can redeem the passes only after checking in to H&H and spending $5 at Kelly's Coffee or Auntie Anne's pretzels.	
The Mint (Los Angeles music venue)	Receive 2-for-1 well drinks, draft beer, or wine on every check-in.	
Ripley's Believe It or Not! Museum (Hollywood)	Popular tourist attraction that rewards first-time check-ins with 50 percent off all purchases.	
Wolf Camera (San Francisco Bay Area)	Camera shops that offer five free prints with every check-in.	

183

TABLE 11.4

BAR/CLUB VENUE SPECIAL EXAMPLES

Bar/Club	Special (Incentive)	Mayor Special
Palace Nightclub (Chicago)	Loyalty special. Every fifth check-in, no waiting in line and first drink is free.	Mayor always receives first drink free (beer, wine, or well).
Pig 'N Whistle (Hollywood bar)	First-time check-ins are rewarded with $5 Don 'Q Rum cocktails.	
SPARC SF (San Francisco cannabis club)	A smokin' deal in this San Francisco cannabis club: get 50 percent off the house blend kief on every third check-in.	
The Vanguard (Hollywood nightclub)		The mayor receives VIP treatment every night. The mayor and guest do not pay a cover, and the first drink is on the house.
Hollmann Salon (Vienna)	Get a free cup of coffee or glass of Prosecco for every check-in.	
Millennium Biltmore Hotel (Los Angeles)	Get 15 percent off any appetizer at the Gallery Bar with proof of a check-in.	

184

TABLE 11.5

RESTAURANT VENUE SPECIAL EXAMPLES

Restaurant	Special (Incentive)	Mayor Special
BLT Burger (New York burger joint)	Free draft beer with any burger upon check-in.	Free burger.
Blu LA Café (Los Angeles restaurant)	Receive 10 percent off your bill on every third check-in.	
Brasserie Julien (New York restaurant)	Free cocktail with every check-in.	
Cafe Zazo (San Francisco restaurant)	Check in and get a medium latte for the price of a small.	
Checkers/Rally's (American hamburger chain)	Free small milkshake on every third check-in.	Free small milkshake on every visit.
Chili's Grill & Bar (bar & restaurant chain)	Receive free chips and salsa on every check-In.	
Crumbs (East Coast cupcake chain)	Free medium iced coffee with every check-in on Fridays only.	
Domino's Pizza (London)		Domino's Pizza locations reward the mayor of each restaurant with a small pizza every Wednesday.
Gabriela's Restaurant and Tequila Bar (New York Mexican restaurant)	Free 8 oz. frozen margarita on third check-in.	
Green Rock Tap & Grill (Hoboken, New Jersey)		The mayor never goes hungry. An order of free wings is always waiting for the mayor upon arrival.

185

continued

TABLE 11.5

RESTAURANT VENUE SPECIAL EXAMPLES, *continued*

Restaurant	Special (Incentive)	Mayor Special
Houlihan's (Indianapolis restaurant chain)	Free mini-dessert for checking in.	First-time mayors get a $25 gift certificate.
Hummus Bros (London restaurant)		The mayor is the king at this restaurant on London's South Hampton Row. Show the waiter that you're the mayor, and enjoy two main courses for the price of one—for you and a friend.
La Paella (New York restaurant)	Free glass of sangria with every check-in Sunday to Thursday.	
The Mermaid Inn (New York seafood restaurant)	Check in to claim a free side item.	Dethrone the mayor, and receive a free lobster sandwich.
McCormick & Schmick's (national seafood restaurant)	Check in during happy hour, and receive one free food item from the bar menu with purchase of any beverage.	
Pizza Hut		Free order of breadsticks with purchase of large pizza.
Spring Street Smoke House (Los Angeles BBQ restaurant)	Check in for the first time and get a free iced tea, lemonade, or fountain soda.	
Swagat (Tokyo tapas restaurant)		The mayor just shows his or her phone to the manager and gets the first drink of beer, wine, or soda free.

Restaurant	Special (Incentive)	Mayor Special
Tat's Delicatessen (Seattle, Washington)		Free sandwich for the mayor on the 16th of every month.
Tokyo Curry Lab (Tokyo's #1 curry house)	Get a free fried egg with your first check-in.	
The 24/7 Restaurant at the Standard Hotel (Los Angeles)	Receive a free dessert with the purchase of any entrée after your third check-in.	
Vapiano (restaurant chain with several locations around Frankfurt, Germany)		*Der Mayor bekommt bei jedem Besuch eine Kaffeespezialität aufs Haus.* (Mayor gets a free coffee special every time he or she enters the restaurant.)
The Westin Austin at the Domain (Austin, Texas)	Anyone who checks in enjoys a complimentary glass of Trefethen late-harvest Riesling after the meal.	

187

Remember, these specials are just a snapshot—one moment in a day on foursquare. They most certainly will change and become even more robust as businesses get more creative. Most of the deals in these tables are intended to incentivize customers to check in for the first time and return to the establishment by rewarding them for loyal behavior. Encouraging foursquare users to check in can work for most businesses, brands, and local merchants. But the best incentives are attention grabbing—they give people a reason to return and encourage those users to share the experience with their friends. Small business owners are now limited only by the scope of their ambition and the extent of their creativity.

Treat Mayors Like Royalty, but Give Everyone a Seat at the Table

Businesses are finding that a mix of rewards for the mayor and specials for everyone else results in the most effective campaigns. Tropical Smoothie Café is a chain of franchised fruit-juice bars that began as a small business with one store in Tallahassee, Florida. In a little more than a decade, it has grown to more than 300 locations. The chain ran two four-square tests to see which campaign had the most success: a check-in special for everyone or a reward for the mayor only.

For one month Tropical Smoothie offered the mayors of its test locations a 50 percent discount on any smoothie, limited to one per day. During the same time period they tested a special at other locations. Anyone who checked in, regardless of whether or not he or she was the mayor, received an extra supplement. Supplements, such as the Energize, which fights fatigue, or the Stress Defense, which boosts immunity, range in price from 50 to 75 cents. Although these are not big-ticket items, the incentive worked very well.

Those locations that offered check-in specials for everyone saw a much larger increase in total check-ins, foot traffic, and sales than the venues that offered mayor-only rewards. Here's the theory—Tropical Smoothie Cafés are typically located in strip malls near grocery stores. A foursquare user check-ing in at the grocery store next door would see the Tropical Smoothie special pop up on his or her phone. Now think about it. If you discover that a nearby juice bar is offering a discount for only the mayor—and you haven't earned the title—there is very little incentive for you to visit the store if you had not planned to do so. But if you open your phone while you're in the grocery store and see a special for a "free" supplement at the juice bar next door, you are more likely to visit the store before walking to your car. Tropical Smoothie discovered that it could successfully reach its fans and poten-tial customers wherever they were—whether they were in the juice bar, outside the store, or in a completely different establishment nearby. The lesson: treat your mayor like royalty, but give everyone a seat at the table.

Why We Can't Turn Down a Freebie

Small businesses and local merchants can find power in foursquare because there's power in the word *free*. In *Free: How Today's Smartest Businesses Profit by Giving Something for Nothing*, Chris Anderson recounts a story that introduced the most powerful marketing tool of the twentieth century—the story of Jell-O. In 1895, Pearle Wait was trying to figure out how to sell a new creation: prepackaged, flavored gelatin. His wife renamed the colorful, light, and jiggly concoction, calling it Jell-O. Wait struggled with marketing and gave up two years later, selling the rights to businessman Frank Woodward for $450.

Woodward came up with the ingenious idea of giving away Jell-O recipes for free—not the Jell-O, but the recipes. The company's salesmen at the time could not sell door-to-door without a costly license, but giving away recipes for free wasn't "selling." Instead of giving out the product, they gave away free information that could be unlocked only by buying the product. Jell-O sales hit one million dollars by 1906, a fortune in those times. "Thus was born one of the most powerful marketing tools of the twentieth century: giving away one thing to create demand for another,"[4] writes Anderson. Woodward understood that *"free* is a word with an extraordinary ability to reset consumer psychology, create new markets, break old ones, and make almost any product more attractive."

Location-based marketing tools are simply the twenty-first-century version of Woodward's free recipes. Woodward quickly learned that free doesn't mean profitless. Anderson argues that you can make money from the concept of free. "Free opens doors, reaching new consumers. People will pay to save time. They will pay for quality. They will pay to lower

189

their risk. They will pay for things they love. They will pay for status." People will pay for your service or your product if it improves their lives. All they need is an incentive to give your business a try.

UNLOCK THE POWER

- **Visit foursquare.com and select "Merchants."** This link will guide you through the process of claiming your venue as well as explaining each of the specials available.
- **Experiment with all types of specials.** Be creative and have fun. A merchant or manager can create several different specials to attract new customers. These go by the following names: Swarm, Friends, Flash, Newbie, and Check-in. Foursquare offers two other specials to reward loyal customers: the Mayor special and the Loyalty special. Each of these options is available for free after you claim your venue.
- **Create specials that incentivize behavior for both mayors and others.** Consider your venue's surroundings and your brand position as you develop a foursquare strategy. For example, if you own a restaurant near a football stadium, you might encourage wearing the team's colors on game days for patrons to unlock a special. There are endless possibilities to the creative incentives you can offer.

CHAPTER 12

Local Heroes

"Foursquare, along with other social media tools, helps you maintain an ongoing conversation with your customers."

—**TRACY MARKS,** Public Relations Specialist, Souplantation & Sweet Tomatoes

How to unlock the Local badge
Check in to the same location three times in one week.

When foursquare users check in to a store, restaurant, or other location, they share this activity with their friends. Savvy businesses are learning that by giving these users an incentive to patronize their establishments, the viral nature of the platform leads to additional (and free) digital impressions and conversations. An incentive redeemed once might translate into hundreds, or thousands, of short bursts of conversation, raising awareness of the venue among a highly desirable demographic. In this chapter you'll learn about a chain of salad bars encouraging customer loyalty by adding a mobile marketing layer to its existing social media efforts. You will also hear directly from a former high-tech executive who is using location-based services to introduce an old pizza chain to a new generation of diners.

A Sweet Incentive

SOUPLANTATION & SWEET TOMATOES
San Diego, California

When a salad bar has 68,000 Facebook fans you know the place must make one heck of a salad. Souplantation & Sweet Tomatoes was founded in 1978 in San Diego, California, and has grown to more than 118 buffet-style restaurants in 15 states. The restaurant's signature salad bar is an all-you-care-to-eat selection of soups, salads, muffins, focaccia, breads, and desserts.

The company has a significant Facebook and Twitter presence. Foursquare came to the company's attention when Tracy

Marks, Souplantation & Sweet Tomatoes' public relations and social media specialist, downloaded it to her phone to check it out. She was surprised to discover that people were already checking in to the chain and that most locations even had a mayor! In other words, Souplantation customers were already using the software but *not being rewarded* for their loyalty. It became clear to Marks that foursquare was a logical extension of the brand's social media initiative because it brings a virtual audience into physical stores. According to Marks, "We saw foursquare as a great guest engagement piece to our social media efforts."[1] Marks pitched the idea of a foursquare campaign to her director of marketing, who readily approved it because there was "no real downside and no dollar investment."

Foursquare Strategy in 40 Restaurants

The company's foursquare strategy launched in October 2010 across 10 Souplantation locations in San Diego. As the number of weekly check-ins began to climb, the company expanded the test to all 40 restaurants in Southern California. The company kept the incentive simple and significant. The special read:

> Thanks for checking in at Souplantation. Show your phone to the cashier for 15 percent off lunch or dinner.

The company made sure all of the cashiers understood the special by sending a voice mail to every store manager, a memo that showed a photo of the campaign, and most important for the employees—a promo code included in the text of the offer. Cashiers simply had to choose the code in their point-of-sale (POS) systems.

Within five months, foursquare discount codes had been redeemed nearly 1,000 times just in the select locations participating in the experiment. But as you've learned by now, the real power of foursquare comes from sharing and recommending. Those Souplantation customers who checked in to unlock the special often chose to automatically share their check-ins with Twitter and Facebook friends. Today a foursquare user near a participating Souplantation location will see the special in a list of specials nearby, and if that person uses the Explore feature, foursquare might recommend Souplantation for a number of reasons, not the least of which is that it is popular with foursquare users.

Souplantation considers the experiment a success and plans to expand its foursquare promotion to all its restaurants. Some Souplantation locations, especially in Los Angeles, are seeing 500 to 1,000 check-ins a week with *no incentive or reward* being offered. The company quickly realized that it's time to extend the specials to all of its customers.

Having Conversations with Loyal Customers

According to Marks, "Our company sees foursquare as a great avenue to reach a new audience. For example, we have a strong online presence with our e-mail guest loyalty program called Club Veg, which has 1.5 million members. Younger and tech-savvy smartphone users who might not be members of our e-mail club will now get discount incentives just for walking through the doors of a Souplantation & Sweet Tomatoes."

Marks says many customers are pleasantly surprised to walk in, check in, and get an unexpected discount. As a bonus, these are the type of diners who are more likely to share the information with their friends. Souplantation's marketing staff takes it one step further and engages these foursquare fans on Facebook and Twitter, creating an even greater loyalty loop and incentivizing its customers to drop in again. Here's an example of one Twitter conversation:

> **@cosibar:** Souplantation 21309 Hawthorne Blvd gives 15% discount when you check in with your foursquare app.
> **@souplantation:** do you like our @foursquare specials? We hope so. Was it a surprise?
> **@cosibar:** @souplantation. Yep . . . A nice surprise! Thx.

As the public relations and social media specialist for Souplantation, Marks plays an active role in having

CHECKING IN

"Get out there and start testing. See what your consumers enjoy. Foursquare and other social media tools can help you keep on an ongoing conversation with your customers."

—**TRACY MARKS,** Public Relations/Social Media Specialist, Souplantation & Sweet Tomatoes

---

conversations with her loyal customers where they are living their lives, often on social networks. She uses Twitter to communicate with the mayors of each location and asks them for their suggestions regarding what types of rewards the restaurants should give its mayors. Suggestions have ranged from free food to reserved tables. Mayors like to be treated like royalty, and they like it when others know it, too!

"We see an increase of awareness of our restaurants on Twitter because of all the people checking in to our locations on Twitter and sharing their check-ins," says Marks. "We've been using this as an opportunity to start a conversation with these guests, asking them their opinions on menu items, for instance. Ideally, we try to reach them when they are still in the location. They love it when we do!"

(195)

Foursquare Gives an Old Pizza Chain a Fresh Start

 STRAW HAT PIZZA
San Ramon, California

I have fond memories of growing up in San Jose, California, and going to Straw Hat Pizza after soccer games. My dad never missed a game, and he would bring me to the local pizza parlor where we would meet up with other players and coaches. The restaurant was colorful, fun, and lively, and had tasty pizza. Straw Hat had been around well before I discovered it. In the summer of 1959, when Frankie Avalon topped the charts and Sandra Dee played Gidget in the first beach party movie, *Pacific Coast Highway,* California was dotted with convertibles, drive-throughs, and young kids playing on the sand and rocking out to the Beach Boys. California was sexy and so was its food. Straw Hat was the first to introduce the Genuine California Pizza. Lighter in style than its counterparts in Chicago, it was made with a layered, flaky crust, light and zesty tomato sauce, fresh toppings with California-style ingredients, and six types of naturally aged California cheeses. It was on the cutting edge of a taste trend that would last for the next five decades.

A Company with a Great History

By the mid-80s, Straw Hat was regarded as one of the dominant pizza chains in the western United States. In 1987, Pizza Hut bought all existing corporate-owned Straw Hats as part of its western expansion plan and ended the chain's reign. I moved on to college in Southern California and completely lost touch with the great pizza and community atmosphere I remembered as a kid. I recently learned that after the Pizza Hut buyout, a few stubborn Straw Hat franchise owners refused to convert and won the right to carry the brand name forward. But for the next 20 years, the Straw Hat Pizza name was all but forgotten, with the exception of a few mom-and-pop stores scattered around northern California.

In February 2008, former high-tech executive Jonathan Fornaci was named president and CEO of Straw Hat Restaurants. He had an uphill climb. Fornaci took over a company with 38 restaurants that were showing little to no growth, did little to no advertising, and did not engage in any social media programs. But Fornaci told me he felt right at home. "It was a company that had a great history, family-oriented atmosphere, and quality products. It had the foundation to be a 450-store chain again like it was in the 1980s. All it needed was new leadership with a vision to build on the foundation that made it great."[2]

In the next three years, in the middle of a great recession, Fornaci grew the brand by 250 percent and has positioned the chain for aggressive expansion over the next several years. According to Fornaci, Straw Hat has a story to tell, a story that he decided to tell on Facebook, Twitter, and foursquare.

Straw Hat hired Fornaci to grow the chain—not slowly, but quickly. Fornaci realized he had to reconnect the brand with customers like me who remembered the brand and, at the same time, introduce the brand to our kids. People like me would remember the brand, but the challenge would be to connect with kids, teens, and young adults who had no recollection of the old magic. Fornaci needed to reach an entire generation of patrons ranging in age from 10 to 25 years old, and he would reach them where they were having conversations on social media networks. But first he had to have a story to tell. Fornaci tapped into three areas where he thought the pizza parlor could differentiate itself and raise awareness with Generation Y and their parents: ingredients, community, and mobile social media.

197

Three Steps to Generation Y

If a pizza doesn't taste good, no amount of social media will make a difference. So Fornaci made sure the pizzas were made with fresh produce grown and shipped within 150 miles of each restaurant, naturally aged California cheeses, and flour ingredients sourced from the company's own wheat fields.

The next step was to turn the restaurants into destinations. "If you coach a Little League or soccer team, where can you go within a few miles of your house to have good food, have fun, and be entertained all at a reasonable price?" Fornaci asked. He turned Straw Hat into exactly that kind of experience. Straw Hat parlors are now family (and team) friendly with upgraded decors, large-screen TVs, arcades, game rooms, televisions in each booth, and TVs with digital memory card slots so kids can see the photographs of their game while enjoying their pizza.

The third step in Straw Hat's transformation was entering the world of social media. "Every one of those kids is on their smartphone, and we needed to connect with them where they were living their lives," says Fornaci. He started by making sure every store had Wi-Fi: "Parents might not care, but the kids get mad if they can't talk to their friends on Facebook." Fornaci established a Facebook page and a Twitter account; however, foursquare was the vehicle that really sparked the creative fire in this former tech executive. "I learned about foursquare because I'm always reading and keeping up with new things," says Fornaci. "It's what I used to do in my venture capital days. I always want to know what's out there, and foursquare fit right in."

Foursquare fit in to Fornaci's vision because it was fun and it reached his customers where they were sharing and giving information—not in the newspaper but on their smartphones. According to Fornaci, "The convenience factor is huge for this generation. Nobody wants to go back to the old ways of clipping coupons. With smartphones and foursquare, they can get all the benefits of those coupons and have more fun. Our specials offer customers a strong incentive to visit our restaurants. It's convenient, easy, and encourages loyalty. It's also free. Why wouldn't you do it?"

Fornaci is a big believer in "shock value." Asking someone to clip a coupon for the same dull incentives that most pizza chains offer would not translate well to the mobile platform. Fornaci realized that smartphone users want to be surprised, so he surprised them in a big way. For example, most chains might offer a free drink for the purchase of a pizza. Fornaci turned the tables, offering a free pizza for the purchase of a drink. "You've got to shock people in a recession," says Fornaci. "Most coupons in mailers give you $1 off a small or $2 off a large pizza. You see the same thing all the time. But our special made people notice. You may never have tried Straw Hat Pizza, but if you only have to pay $1.79 for a drink to get a free pizza, why not try it?"

Fornaci hired a social media professional to work with franchise owners to offer fresh, creative, and shocking specials

CHECKING IN

> *"Use all multiple social media platforms, including Facebook,*
> *Twitter, and foursquare. Set up foursquare yourself to see just*
> *how easy it is to use. It takes about 30 minutes to get your store*
> *on foursquare. The entire process is very simple. Even if you're not*
> *tech-savvy, you can have a weekly promotion up in no time. It's*
> *not like writing HTML code or creating a Web page. It's the easiest*
> *possible thing to do. And it's free. Why wouldn't you do it?"*

—**JONATHAN FORNACI,**
President and CEO, Straw Hat Restaurants

that change frequently. Restaurant owners could easily offer day-only or special-event specials to encourage diners to choose Straw Hat over another pizza joint or restaurant. For example, on the day of the Super Bowl in January 2011, Straw Hat got people in the door by offering instant foursquare specials like beer for 75 cents or six chicken wings for a buck (items that typically cost $3 to $4).

According to Fornaci, "The big advantage with foursquare is that every store can offer its own specials based on their demographics. Local owners know their communities best. We want to allow the franchise owner to figure out what incentives make the most sense in their local markets. For example, let's say the local high school just won a championship. A Straw Hat owner could create a special: wear the high school colors and get a free personal pizza."

Data Doesn't Lie

Fornaci is a big believer in the power of mobile marketing to replace traditional methods of distributing coupons and promotions. "It's a huge savings for individual restaurants," says Fornaci. "We've done a ton of promotions like door hangers and direct mail pieces. An insert in a Sunday newspaper is very, very expensive, and you're lucky to get a 2 to 4 percent return rate. An individual owner can easily spend $2,000 to $4,000 on advertising, and for what? A 2 percent hit rate? It costs you nothing with foursquare."

Fornaci shared some data with me, individual store statistics from Super Bowl Sunday that surprised the both of us. The Excel spreadsheet showed three columns for each of the Straw Hat stores in a vicinity from Salinas to Sacramento, California (50 stores in all). The columns were labeled: eClub redeemed (coupons sent by e-mail), FB redeemed (coupons delivered to Facebook fans), and 4sq redeemed (foursquare). During the Super Bowl, Straw Hat offered the same general incentives on Facebook, through e-mail, and via foursquare— discounts on wings, beer, and pizza. Customers had to print the e-mail coupons, and they had to show their phone to redeem the foursquare promotion. Some locations on the outskirts of large towns saw only 1 foursquare redemption, while others saw more than 30 redemptions during the Super Bowl.

As we reviewed each cell in the spreadsheet, we discovered that nearly all the restaurants posted the most redemptions in the foursquare column. In fact, the redemption rate was significantly higher for foursquare than it was for either Facebook or e-mailed coupons. Fifty-four percent of the total redemptions came from foursquare, 30 percent from the e-mail campaign, and 16 percent from Facebook. In most cases, individual Straw Hat Restaurants saw up to nine foursquare redemptions for every one redemption in the other categories. Out of 50 stores, only 3 had higher e-mail redemptions than foursquare or Facebook redemptions. And those stores were located in remote areas that had poor phone reception, so it's quite likely that there were few customers in the area who were actively using their smartphones. Here's the bottom line: across 50 Straw Hat locations in California, foursquare was more effective in generating business than both e-mails and Facebook. Foursquare brought in *16 percent* more customers than both e-mail and Facebook coupons *combined*.

Foursquare—a free service—brought more people through the door than other digital and social media promotions. Individual franchise owners could also access the foursquare merchant dashboard for a rich data set of information, including: number of check-ins per day, time of day when the most check-ins occur, how many check-ins share information with Twitter and Facebook, gender and age breakdowns, and most loyal customers. Individual franchise owners can also use foursquare's merchant tools to create and manage their own specials.

Straw Hat's Super Bowl foursquare promotion convinces Fornaci that he's on the right track, successfully connecting with a new generation of customers. Despite Straw Hat's impressive growth, Foranci has a long road ahead if he hopes to bring Straw Hat back to its glory days. But as long as his customers have foursquare in their pockets, Fornaci has a direct line to their hearts. Would you bet against him?

🔓 UNLOCK THE POWER

- ◆ **Extend the conversation.** Promote your foursquare specials on Twitter and Facebook. The full power of foursquare is unleashed in combination with an overall social media strategy.
- ◆ **Shock and awe.** Take the Straw Hat approach—give people the unexpected. If they expect a free drink with a pizza, give them a free pizza with a drink just for checking in. You can always turn off the special if it's too successful!

CHAPTER 13

Never Stop Entertaining

You can't get away from it. Foursquare by its very nature is playful!

—**NAVEEN SELVADURAI,** Cofounder, foursquare

Every week millions of television viewers around the world check in with wealthy "housewives" in Atlanta, Orange County, Beverly Hills, and several other cities in the United States. The Real Housewives franchise has become a monster success for the cable network that airs it—Bravo. The cable network's official Twitter site boasts more than 80,000 followers. Bravo's foursquare page attracted more than 117,000 fans in less than one year.

Bravo's programming is centered around five passion points: food, fashion, beauty, design, and pop culture. Its shows attract an upscale and educated cable audience. They are also very tech savvy. Bravo's vice president of marketing, Ellen Stone, told me that her marketing team is constantly searching for new innovations and decided to launch the first branded experience on foursquare.

Even "30 Rock" Has a Mayor

Stone and her team scour newspapers, blogs, and online sources to see what might be relevant to their television audience. One day they came across a story about a start-up called foursquare that, at the time, had 87,000 users. Since Bravo employees represent the Bravo audience, Stone took the simple step of asking them about foursquare—had they heard of it? Not only had they heard of it, many were active users, bragging about their mayorships. Even Bravo's head-quarters at "30 Rock" had a mayor. That was all the proof she needed. Stone challenged her team: how do we use this new social media outlet to engage our audience? According to Stone, "The Bravo viewers are very tech forward. They are early adopters and trendsetters. We wanted to take the Bravo programming and create a deeper level of engagement by having the experience continue off the TV screen."[1] Any campaign would have to accomplish two things: promote Bravo's unique content and bring enjoyment to its viewers. The campaign had to be fun!

Building Buzz Bravolebrities Would Love

Bravo's first foursquare campaign kicked off in January 2009 and was intended to build buzz—for Bravo and foursquare. Bravo created custom badges associated with shows like "Top Chef." Users could also unlock a Bravo Newbie badge or a Fashionista badge by visiting beauty retailer Sephora. Bravo promoted the partnerships on the air and offered promotions and specials. For example, the first people to unlock the Newbie badge would receive Flip camcorders, Bravo umbrellas, and other prizes. Of the first 10 people who unlocked the badges, 5 were bloggers. They wrote about the promotion and started an entirely new digital stream about foursquare. Bravo discovered that foursquare's "amplification factor" was high. But the badges, while successful at creating buzz, were just the beginning.

Bravo offers city guides available for download on its website (http://guides.bravotv.com/guides/new_york). The guides offer a Bravo-approved list of restaurants, shopping, and nightlife venues. The guides also include a list of venues that Bravolebrities would frequent. The stars of Bravo's popular shows are dubbed Bravolebrities, and they are the ones who populate the tips and to-dos at their favorite venues. This provides a unique opportunity for viewers of, say, the "Rachel Zoe Project" to visit the same fashion-focused boutiques and locations while experiencing their own "OMG" moments.

Shortly after the partnership with foursquare, Bravo saw a 31 percent increase in the digital downloads of these guides on the Bravo iPhone application. This application engages viewers after the shows when they are outside their living rooms and in the real world. The app offers a fun way to keep Bravo's content fresh on the minds of a hip, urban audience.

Bravo Brings More than Just Desserts

On September 15, 2010, Bravo devoted a social media campaign to drive publicity for and to celebrate the premier of a new show called "Top Chef: Just Desserts," a spin-off of the hugely successful show "Top Chef." The program aired right after the "Top Chef" season seven finale. The campaign covered New York, Chicago, Los Angeles, and more than one dozen other cities. Retailers whose venues had been tagged by Bravo in those cities participated in the campaign, offering free desserts for foursquare users who checked in. Bravo also rewarded users who checked in with a special Just Desserts badge. The unlocked text read:

> It's time to get your sweet on! Show this badge and enjoy today's FREE dessert offer. And don't miss the premiere of "Just Desserts" tonight on BRAVO at 11/10c.

The free dessert offer was valid from 1:00 to 3:00 P.M. at more than 200 dessert shops and participating venues across the country. Many of the shops were celebrating with "Just Desserts" themed parties. Bravo posted a list of participating eateries on its Facebook page. "In some places the lines were literally around the block," says Stone. The campaign generated its own viral component because many users who unlocked Bravo badges also notified their friends and followers on Twitter. Here's an example of a Twitter post from the day of the campaign:

> I got my Top Chef Just Desserts Day Hat! Can't wait for finale and Just Desserts premier tonight on Bravo. Xoxo Denise10283.

In June 2010, Bravo continued with the badge-themed campaigns, this time in partnership with Sephora for four weeks in the tri-state area (New Jersey, New York, and Connecticut). The reward included a Sephora $100 gift card for users who unlocked the Real Housewife badge. Again, the network received far more publicity than expected, because of the viral nature of foursquare and its fan base. Bloggers began writing about the promotion, and people were sharing the information with their Facebook and Twitter friends. Thanks to extended digital dialogue, Bravo added 10,000 friends in a few weeks.

Foursquare and Bravo "Hook Up" for New Year's Eve

On New Year's Eve 2010, Bravo launched a successful foursquare campaign for its inaugural special, Andy Cohen's New Year's Eve Party. Bravo streamed live profile photos, first names, and hometowns of foursquare users who follow Bravo and checked in that night.

"We were getting two or three check-ins every second during Andy's show," says Stone. In addition, Bravo saw hundreds of tweets during the show, shared by users who were excited to either see their names or be a part of the promotion.

According to Stone, "The badges, rewards, and promotions have all been a clear win-win for foursquare and Bravo." Mobile marketing on foursquare has been a clear winner for Bravo because the network is always looking for opportunities to align its content and brand with new and current viewers. As an entertainment brand, Bravo instinctively understands that the real power of foursquare is unlocked when a promotion is fun, whimsical, and entertaining.

As of this writing, Bravo has eight branded badges (Bravo Newbie, Real Housewife, Fashionista, and others). Stone says that Bravo will continue to experiment with foursquare promotions because "foursquare holds a special place in our hearts."

207

CHECKING IN

"As a business owner, you need to know your 'audience,' your customer. Don't copy Bravo. Our audience is different than yours. Create rewards that mean something to your audience."

—**ELLEN STONE,** Senior Vice President of Marketing, Bravo TV

Facilitating Serendipity

One of my first conversations for this book took place with an early investor in foursquare who said he loves the service because it brings unexpected and playful moments in his life. He told me the story of the night he first unlocked the School Night badge (unlocked when you check in after 3:00 A.M. on a "school night," Sunday through Thursday). He had spent a long—and presumably happy—night of bar-hopping in the city even though he had an early morning meeting the next day. He dragged himself into the meeting, and his bleary eyes caught the eyes of his friend who had been following his exploits on foursquare. She gave him a knowing smile, and they both laughed about it later.

Foursquare cofounder Dennis Crowley says moments like these are examples of foursquare facilitating serendipity; badges, leaderboards, mayorships, tips, and specials make your world more fun to explore. A business that considers location-based mobile services as just another tool to push coupons to customers will be missing out on the real benefit of these tools to connect with and to engage its customers on a much deeper level than ever before.

Deliver Joyful Moments

When Apple first introduced the iPad, skeptics were plentiful. Many observers, bloggers, and writers posed the question, "Why would someone want a third device in between a laptop and a smartphone?" Shortly after the iPad became available, I was walking out of a coffee shop and saw a small group of about five elementary-school-age girls laughing and giggling as they huddled around a device on the table. I glanced over and noticed they were playing with the new iPad. I thought to myself, "Anything that brings that much joy to people's lives will be a winner." Sure enough, it was a winner. In less than one year the iPad had sold 15 million units. In 2011 more than 100 competitors had been introduced to the market, but few garnered more favorable reviews than Apple's next generation of tablets—the iPad 2.

What had the skeptics missed? They didn't see the joy that people were experiencing when they used the product. I saw a very similar trend with foursquare and the checking-in revolution. Many reporters failed to see the value in it because they were not active users at the time they wrote their stories. Once foursquare began growing by a million new users a month, the headlines began to change. Reporters went from asking, "Why would people care about becoming a virtual mayor?" to proclaiming that "your business needs to be on foursquare." Again, what had the skeptics missed? They missed seeing people walk around the city of New York or popular festivals like South by Southwest sporting temporary foursquare badge tattoos. They missed the story about a Tampa eye doctor voluntarily starting foursquare Day and turning it into a worldwide celebration. They missed the mayor—the real mayor—of Austin, Texas, proclaiming April 16 as foursquare Day. They missed the experience of restaurant owners and local merchants around the world who revitalized their businesses thanks to reaching new, mobile customers. And they certainly couldn't understand why anyone would check in to a venue to earn a badge or become a mayor and share the achievement with their friends. People do it because it's fun. It's a game. It brings them joy and sometimes even love.

209

A foursquare Love Story

Dwayne Kilbourne met his girlfriend, Elaine Jackson, at the gym. Now you might think there's nothing unusual about that—people meet at the gym all the time. In many cases, that's why they go! The story of how Dwayne met Elaine has a little twist. They met on foursquare. Both were working out at the same gym, an LA Fitness club in Kenneshaw, Georgia, about 30 minutes north of Atlanta.

Dwayne was new to town, and since he was an avid foursquare user, he decided to use the software to explore nearby venues. Little did Dwayne know foursquare was about to facilitate serendipity in a way that would change his life. On June 19, 2010, Dwayne noticed that a beautiful lady named Elaine was also checking in to his club on foursquare. He sent a friend request to Elaine. She accepted, and the rest is a foursquare love story.

About a month later Dwayne and Elaine had their first date, which they spent hiking at the Kenneshaw Mountain National Battlefield Park, a park that covers about 3,000 acres of land that was the site of a Civil War battle. I learned this piece of dating trivia because it's a tip they left at the venue. Since both Dwayne and Elaine are avid foursquare users, they did the next natural thing—they created a branded foursquare page to share their stories with others. Visit http://foursquare .com/4sqlovestory, and you'll find a page that is part tour guide, part diary, and part love story. For example, if you visit the Georgia Aquarium, you might see this message pop up on your phone:

> Elaine treats Dwayne to his first trip here on 3/12/2011. It's no wonder this place is so popular—an awesome array of aquatic animals makes it a must-see place!

If you're watching a Braves game at Turner Field, you might see this piece of trivia about the time Elaine took Dwayne here to see his first Braves game:

> Turner Field Section 239. We sat in this section in right field. We must say that this is a great spot to sit if you like seeing the entire field and also the Braves' bullpen.

And of course, if you do happen to be at or near the LA Fitness club in Kenneshaw, Georgia, you might come across this message:

> We realized that we both worked out here (first meet up = 7/18/10 at leg press machine)—all thanks to foursquare.

Dwayne and Elaine are both social media junkies, so sharing their story is second nature. You can follow their foursquare love story on their blog, on Twitter, Facebook, and foursquare, as well as watching their videos on YouTube. People like Dwayne and Elaine are your customers. They're falling in love with their smartphones and the serendipitous moments those smartphones enable. If you engage them, they'll fall in love with you.

Look Your Best, Bro

On January 6, 2011, gyms, tanning salons, and laundromats around the United States could tap into the success of MTV's "Jersey Shore" to help their customers unlock the four-square GTL badge. Fans of the popular show know that one tanned and muscular cast member—Mike "The Situation" Sorrentino—likes to make sure that he has his GTL on. In Jersey speak, GTL stands for "gym, tanning, and laundry," the three things that Mike says a guy should do every day. Mike says that "gotta GTL every day to make sure you're looking your best, bro. If your shirt looks bad, it makes the whole product look bad."

Foursquare users who followed MTV could unlock the GTL badge by checking into a gym, tanning salon, or laundromat in the same week. The text read:

> Fresh to death! You've checked in for the GTL. Don't miss the new season of the "Jersey Shore"—Thursdays at 10P/9C on MTV. Now pump that fist and dodge those grenades!"

If you watch "Jersey Shore" you know what a "grenade" is. If you don't, you probably wouldn't care anyway. Serious critics hate "Jersey Shore," but it's one of the most popular shows on television because it's vicarious fun and MTV knows it. The network had fun with the foursquare badge. Across the country some gym owners, tanning salons, and laundromats played along and got in on the act. The owner of Extreme Tan and Smoothies in Florida offered his own foursquare specials and blogged about the new GTL badge, enticing people to check in to one of his six Tampa-area locations.

The owner—"Extreme" John—calls himself a social media addict. He maintains a blog, as well as personal and brand Twitter and Facebook pages. Now he's adding foursquare to the mix in a creative and fun way.

By its nature, social media is fun. You will miss an incredible opportunity if you forget that mobile social networking

CHECKING IN

Help your customers achieve their "merit" badges. Look closely at foursquare's badges. If they look familiar, it's because they were inspired by Boy and Girl Scout merit badges. Scouts have more than 100 merit badges they can attain, but they must do something to earn those badges. For example, a young Boy Scout can earn the aviation badge by visiting an airport and giving a report to his scout leader, or he can earn the computer badge by creating a blog about his scouting activities. Girl Scout merit badges work in much the same way. From Brownies to Girl Scouts, earning badges is an important rite of passage. Young girls can learn more about everything from camping to cooking to computers. As they learn new skills, they earn badges that they wear proudly on their uniforms.

These badges inspired foursquare to create badges that require the user to accomplish something to unlock the badge. Check in to 50 venues to earn the Superstar badge or check in with three members of the opposite sex to earn the Player Please badge. Develop creative ways to help your customers achieve their merits!

is simply an extension of what people already enjoy about existing Internet social media platforms. The reason why foursquare is growing by one million new users a month is because people have fun unlocking badges. They have fun competing for mayor, being rewarded for it, and sharing that experience with friends. Business owners should join the fun, too. Door flyers aren't fun, the Yellow Pages aren't fun, and neither will your foursquare promotion be fun if all you do is push your existing discounts to mobile users.

A club that lets its mayor cut to the front of the line on Friday night is having fun. A restaurant that requires its users to take a photo of a bird, show it to the bartender, and be rewarded with a free drink is having fun. A real estate company that leaves unique tips at iconic establishments in the cities it serves is having fun. A bar and grill that throws foursquare-themed "badge parties" to attract large groups of patrons is having fun. Don't bore your customers. Bring them joy instead. Never stop entertaining them.

(213)

Ken Woos Barbie on foursquare

In case you missed the big news—Ken and Barbie got back together on Valentine's Day, 2011. Dolls are serious business for some grown-up collectors, but for most kids, dolls are strictly for entertainment purposes. Mattel decided to have a lot of fun with the celebrity toy couple who had shocked the world when they split after spending 43 years together. Ken used all forms of social media in his quest to woo Barbie back. He professed his love on billboards in Los Angeles and New York ("Barbie, you are the only doll for me") and with flirtatious posts on his Facebook page. Ken even took to foursquare, checking in at New York City's famous Magnolia Bakery to buy special cupcakes for his beloved. Ken even used his foursquare branded page at http://foursquare.com/officialken to stroll down memory lane. At the Malibu Public Beach, Ken posted this message:

I surprised Barbie with a bonfire and picnic at dusk on Malibu Beach once. I'll never forget how the light flickered off her eyes as we sat and watched the waves crash onto the beach.

Some of Ken's messages also contained tips or recommendations. Foursquare users in the venue of the John Hancock Center in Chicago might come across this post:

Barbie and I had an anniversary dinner at the Signature Room, and the only thing more beautiful than the view atop of Chicago was the girl sitting across from me.

Ken's social media "campaign" worked and once again Barbie was in Ken's arms.

The Ken and Barbie story was all great fun, but the backstory was not nearly as entertaining for Mattel. The company had launched a very serious battle with a former designer who left the company to start the Bratz line of dolls for MGA Entertainment. I was working with Mattel spokespeople during the early days of the lawsuit, and I can tell you that there was nothing fun about it.

The sassy Bratz dolls hit the shelves in 2001, and for the next decade, MGA, the Bratz' owner, sold more than $3 billion in related products. Sales of Barbie, which had become nearly a rite of passage for American girls, slid 15 percent in 2007 and another 12 percent the following year. Mattel alleged that the Bratz decreased Barbie's profits by $390 million. In 2009 a federal jury awarded Mattel $100 million and found that the Bratz designer had indeed developed the concept while working for Mattel. The verdict was later overturned on appeal and retrials, and countersuits continue at the time of this writing.

Mattel says that sales of Barbie have improved considerably thanks, in large part, to her reuniting with Ken and Mattel's aggressive and entertaining social media branding campaign. Ken is not the only celebrity leveraging foursquare to woo followers. One famous chef is cooking up some foursquare ideas of his own.

Mario Batali Cooks up a foursquare Strategy

A social media platform infuses itself in the culture when celebrities jump on board: Ashton Kutcher posting 140-character messages on Twitter and garnering millions of followers, Charlie Sheen broadcasting his rants on uStream, or Lady Gaga earning the title of most popular living celebrity on Facebook. Thanks in large part to growing celebrity awareness of these services, few people in the corporate ranks will question the need to have a presence on Facebook, Twitter, or YouTube in addition to a conventional blog or website. Soon nobody will question a mobile strategy as well.

As a business owner, you will either be paving the road and building followers or waiting until it's much harder for your message to find an audience. Major entertainment brands like MTV and Bravo are validating the brand. Small merchants are joining their ranks by the hundreds of thousands. Individual celebrities are coming next. Conan O'Brien, Stephen Colbert, and Jon Stewart have already played in the foursquare waters, and the list will only continue to grow. The key is to find a way to use the software in a playful, fun, and engaging way. Celebrity chef Mario Batali believes he has found the right ingredients.

Food and wine is one of the most popular check-in categories, so it was fitting that Food Network star Batali would connect his brand with a mobile audience. Wearing his trademark shorts and orange Crocs, Batali travels around the world and leaves foursquare tips at his favorite restaurants or culinary hotspots. If you're near Russ & Daughters Deli on Houston Street in New York City, you might see Batali's tip:

> Best place for smoked fish, caviar, and delicatessen—hands down. Love their whitefish salad!

If you're traveling to Singapore and happen to be near Pizzeria Mozza, you might learn that Batali's favorite pie is the tomato and oregano

Batali has gone beyond offering tips, however. Fans who follow Batali on foursquare (he had 14,000 fans within days of the announcement) also learn about check-in specials at one of Batali's 15 restaurants in New York, Las Vegas, and Los Angeles.

For example, check in during lunch hours to Batali's Otto Enoteca Pizzeria in New York's Greenwich Village, and you can enjoy a free glass of Prosecco with your pizza or pasta. The same deals apply for diners at Batali's Carnevino Italian Steakhouse and B&B Ristorante in Las Vegas. Each of these specials offer small, but powerful, incentives to drop in at one of Batali's restaurants at the very moment the smartphone user is deciding where to eat.

Batali's partnership with foursquare led to the *New York Observer* remarking that foursquare had become the new arbiter of celebrity status. As more celebrities validate the platform, foursquare and other location-based services should continue to grow, and more users will be drawn to their specials and yours, too (remember, your offers appear in the same

CHECKING IN

Foursquare limits your "friends" to 1,000 people. Once you have more than 1,000 friends, foursquare considers you a celebrity. Congratulations! You've made the big time. What this means is that once you hit 1,000 friends, the first 100 will be tagged as "friends" and the rest as followers. This relieves a lot of headaches because the brand or "celebrity" does not get notifications every time someone sends a friend request. Instead, they will be automatically added as followers. This feature provides added quality controls. For example, once a celebrity checks in to a venue, he or she can choose to share those check-ins, shouts, and photos with only friends or with friends and followers as well.

list as more famous restaurants or venues). The foursquare/ Batali partnership makes sense because he is known for creativity, boldness, and a sense of adventure in his culinary techniques and in his restaurants. Follow Batali's lead. Be creative, bold, and adventurous, and have fun doing it!

Chasing "Tail" in New York City

Remember Maria Avgitidis, the fourth-generation matchmaker you met in Chapter 2? Avgitidis credits foursquare as a critical tool for helping her build a personalized New York City dating service. Finding the right match is often a stressful experience, so Maria keeps it light, casual, and above all, fun.

Every year on April 16th (foursquare Day), Maria sponsors a "Bunny Hop" to match single ladies with potential mates. Maria uses Twitter and Facebook to announce the event, but the event itself is purely a foursquare experience. About 100 ladies meet at a bar to get their bunny ears and tail (see Figure 13.1). Together with Maria they stop at several bars during the evening, bars with names like the Thirsty Scholar Pub, Ryan's Irish Pub, and Bull McCabe's. At each venue, the ladies check in, enjoy drink specials, and yes, Maria's male clients "chase the tails" by following Maria on foursquare.

When I first started the research for this book, I thought that check-in services would benefit only those businesses with a physical presence, like bars and restaurants. But then I spent time with the Corcoran Group and learned how leaving whimsical tips throughout New York City benefits their real estate brand. I learned how Maria the data coach built a business on foursquare. I learned how NASA uses foursquare to build awareness for its accomplishments despite not "owning" a physical venue. I learned how a state like Pennsylvania encourages tourism with badges, tips, and specials. I learned how an Oakland nonprofit raised $50,000 for its environmental causes. And I learned how an entertainment brand like Bravo leverages its shows, content, and celebrities to build

FIGURE 13.1

Maria Avgitidis sponsors the "Bunny Hop" every year on foursquare Day.

buzz for its network. The common thread that ties the non-venue brands together: fun. If you can't attract me to a venue with a great deal, then you'd better give me another reason to engage with your brand. And if I'm not entertained, you stand little to no chance of getting my attention and winning my business.

UNLOCK THE POWER

- **Don't take yourself, your specials, or your tips too seriously.** If you're going to leave tips or content, make them fun and whimsical. Here are some examples of the tips the events guide Metromix is leaving at venues in the 60 cities it now covers:

- ◇ **Katz's Deli (Manhattan):** NYC's oldest deli still creates a mean pastrami sandwich, including slow-dried and cured deli meats, briskets, and knockwurst. If anything else, Meg Ryan seems to love it in *When Harry Met Sally.*
- ◇ **Holiday Club (Chicago):** We caught a picture-perfect rendition of the robot, a shirtless man sweating it out Michael Jackson, and an impromptu dance-off between two groups of strangers. All this and 80s jams? Sold!
- ◇ **Dinosaur Bar-B-Que (Manhattan):** Our Readers' Choice WINNER for Best Barbeque. This barbeque joint can bring the "Yabba Dabba Doo" out of you with Fred Flintstone size portions.

- **Have fun with badges.** Foursquare has dozens of unique badges for its users to unlock. Leverage the badges to encourage customers to repeatedly visit your venue. For example, the Local badge is unlocked when a user checks in to the same place three times in one week. Create a Loyalty special that rewards someone for the third check-in and remind that user in the text of the special that he or she can also unlock the badge by checking in to your venue three times in the same week.

- **Look outside your industry for inspiration.** You can learn a lot from a date coach, a state's convention and visitor's bureau, or a television network. Although this book is filled with such case studies that represent nearly every industry, more and more appear every day. Follow my foursquare branded page at http://foursquare.com/carminegallo to keep up with new and exciting stories. The online community Aboutfoursquare.com is a resource that will keep you updated on new partnerships as will foursquare's own blog (http://blog.foursquare.com). In my book *The Innovation Secrets of Steve Jobs*, I talk about how Steve Jobs believes creativity is "connecting things," associating ideas from different fields and applying those ideas to your field. The most creative entrepreneurs look outside their industry for inspiration.

219

CHAPTER 14

Crunked Kings

 We use social media to give people a broader perspective of what we do.

—**STEPHANIE SCHIERHOLZ,** Social Media Manager, NASA

How to unlock the Crunked badge
Check in four different times in
one night.

Foursquare gives everyday people, venues, and local merchants a "voice" according to cofounder Dennis Crowley. Some venues are using this new voice to engage their customers, fans, and followers with creative, fun, and entertaining things to do. In this chapter you'll hear two completely different brand stories—a space agency and a restaurant. One has plenty of money for advertising, and the other doesn't have a dime for marketing (you might be surprised to find out which one has no ad budget). Despite their differences, both are using foursquare creatively to connect with their customers in a whole new way.

Exploring Space on Earth

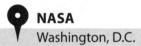

NASA
Washington, D.C.

In 1958, the U.S. Congress created the National Aeronautics and Space Administration (NASA). Its mission was (and continues to be) to pursue activities in space devoted to peaceful purposes for the benefit of all mankind. In the original act that created the agency, Congress also tasked NASA with a mandate to communicate what it does and what it finds. Section 203(a) states that NASA must "provide for the widest practicable and appropriate dissemination of information concerning its activities and the results thereof." The communication clause of the Space Act is one of the most difficult to implement. You see, as a government agency, NASA has no advertising or marketing budget. It turns out that NASA deals with the same challenge facing most small businesses—spreading the word about its great product but not having the ad dollars to do it. What NASA is learning about mobile social marketing, however, applies to all small- and medium-sized businesses that struggle to tell their stories.

When communication budgets are tight or nonexistent, organizations must find creative and innovative ways to get the word out. That's exactly what NASA has done for more than 50 years. For example, video cameras were placed on the Apollo moon missions for two reasons: to show the scientists on Earth what was happening and to dramatically display the story to the rest of the world. Thanks to the video camera placed inside "Quad 4" of the Apollo Lunar Module, we have dramatic images of the first men taking their first steps on the moon. Today NASA continues to have far more advanced color cameras to capture space walks, shuttle launches, and other activities. The space agency even offers NASA TV, devoted to 24 hours a day of streaming video on the Internet and on television.

NASA Launches a Social Media Moon Shot

(223)

In 2009 NASA decided to join Twitter and to communicate with its earthbound followers in 140-character bursts of content. As it turns out, the short posts were a perfect vehicle to send real-time updates of NASA's activities, including links to its popular images of the day or original content. Twitter became far more successful than even its social media managers expected, growing from just a few thousand followers to nearly one million today.

NASA engaged its growing virtual audience with real-world tweetups to spread the word about its missions. Tweetups bring together Twitter users for a behind-the-scenes experience at NASA facilities nationwide. Scientists, engineers, and astronauts meet, talk, and guide the Twitter users, who in turn share the NASA story with millions of followers. As the space shuttle missions were winding down, NASA invited Twitter followers to the Kennedy Space Center in Florida to watch some of the launches. In some cases their tweets reached another two million people. NASA could accommodate only about 150 Twitter fans at the launch site, but those fans reached so many others that it "knocked my socks off," according to NASA social media manager Stephanie Schierholz.

The First Check-In from Space

"I started using foursquare personally to see if there was a natural connection with NASA, if it was something that we should be using,"[1] Schierholz told me. Foursquare's mission is to help you explore your world, so it made sense that it would complement NASA's mission to explore space while introducing people to NASA all around them. "People have a relatively good name awareness of NASA and good feelings about it, but few can articulate everything that NASA does. Yet NASA, its history, and its research are all around them," says Schierholz. "We use social media to connect people with NASA and to give them a broader perspective of what we do."

NASA's branded foursquare page (http://foursquare.com/nasa) has about 80,000 followers and is loaded with hundreds of tips and information for NASA centers, planetariums, museums, and other venues from coast to coast. Here are some samples:

- **Kennedy Space Center Visitor Complex (Merritt Island, Florida):** Your starting point to tour Kennedy, meet astronauts, and train in spaceflight simulators. The complex also is home to an IMAX theater, rocket garden, children's areas, and the U.S. Astronaut Hall of Fame.
- **NASA's Space Center Houston:** Launching point for the popular NASA Tram Tour for a behind-the-scenes look where you could see astronauts training for upcoming missions, the neutral buoyancy lab, and the mission control center.
- **American Museum of Natural History (New York):** The Full Moon exhibition in the Rose Center for Earth and Space contains more than 75 rarely seen photographic prints from NASA's Apollo missions to the moon and are done in both impressive scale and stunning quality.

◆ **Griffith Observatory (Los Angeles):** The 300-seat Oschin Planetarium is one of the finest and most technologically sophisticated in the world. Once a month, Los Angeles astronomy clubs host a free public star party on the lawn.

The foursquare Mission . . . Accomplished!

Schierholz and her social media team at NASA came up with a clever, fun, and entertaining way to introduce the new partnership to earthbound fans. For the promotion they needed the help of a real astronaut, and that's where Douglas "Wheels" Wheelock entered the picture. Wheelock was commander of the International Space Station (ISS) in September 2010 (see Figure 14.1).

During his time on the ISS, Wheelock conducted three space walks and together with other crew members continued work on more than 100 microgravity experiments in research, biology, materials science, technology development, and earth

FIGURE 14.1

Doug Wheelock commanded the International Space Station. Photo courtesy of NASA.

and space sciences (space is a unique environment for scientific experiments because compounds behave differently and processes are accelerated in a zero-gravity environment). Wheelock also had one other critical assignment—he had to check in.

On October 22, 2010, Wheelock became the first person to check in from space. Foursquare partnered with Schierholz and NASA to create a venue page for the ISS. The station itself sits in low orbit 220 miles above the Earth's surface and travels 17,500 miles per hour. As you can imagine, getting a live Internet connection isn't always possible. But it is for about a 10-minute window as the station orbits the world. Wheelock successfully checked in, and by doing so became the first person to unlock NASA's new Explorer badge. Wheelock has his own Twitter account (www.twitter.com/Astro_Wheels), which was connected to his foursquare account. When he unlocked the badge, the message was sent to tens of thousands of Wheelock's followers. The tweet gave those on Earth the cue that he had successfully accomplished the foursquare mission. "It was a huge relief when it worked," says Schierholz. "Now anyone can unlock the badge when they follow NASA on foursquare and check in to NASA and NASA-related locations."

CHECKING IN

"Before you set up a foursquare account for your brand, set up a personal account and use it yourself. The thing about social media is that you can't just read about it. You need to use it. But as you learn how to use it yourself, you can make connections on how it will benefit your brand. Look at what your competitors are doing, what people in your space are doing, and also learn from others who are doing it really well. Then think about how you can apply it to your business."

—**STEPHANIE SCHIERHOLZ,** Social Media Manager, NASA

NASA's work is diverse: proving flight technologies, exploring Earth, exploring the solar system and beyond, developing critical technologies, and conducting scientific experiments in orbit that benefit all of mankind back on Earth. Together with foursquare, NASA has found a mobile partner to help people explore the universe and discover Earth.

A Check-In That's for the Birds

BRYANT PARK GRILL
New York City, New York

The Bryant Park Grill on West 40th Street has been called the crown jewel of New York City's Bryant Park, considered one of New York's loveliest public spaces. Located just behind the New York Public Library, the Grill offers an oasis with a lush setting for lunch, dinner, or after-work drinks. It also has a defining characteristic: its design is based on an aviary. That explains why there is a large bird mural stretching alongside one of the walls.

When the marketing folks at the restaurant were developing a foursquare special, they wanted to create one that held a unique connection to the brand and its surroundings. But they also wanted to have fun. Anyone could offer a foursquare special for 10 percent off a drink at the bar. The Grill's owner decided to create a special that was for the birds, literally.

The Bryant Park Grill foursquare special worked like this: A foursquare user would use his or her smartphone to snap a picture of a bird in Bryant Park. When that user checked in to Bryant Park Grill, he or she would show the photo to any of the bartenders and in return for that simple gesture would be rewarded with a free drink.

The restaurant adapts the special with slightly different twists. For example, instead of a drink, the restaurant will reward a foursquare user with one of its desserts, which, if you read the foursquare tips, shouldn't be missed. But

227

showing a picture of a bird in Bryant Park is still required to earn the reward.

The Bryant Park Grill special incentivizes customers to return for several reasons: It's clever, fun, and unexpected. The Bryant Park Grill special requires you to actively engage with your surroundings. In addition, the special is consistent with its brand and taps into its design, culture, and setting. Since the Grill is conveniently located near Grand Central Station (where thousands of people check in on foursquare), the special offers enough incentive for people to return another day, snap another photograph, and get another bite of the restaurant's famous desserts.

One reviewer said he checked into the restaurant to unlock the foursquare special and thought he was going to have a quick drink and leave. But in one of those serendipitous moments that Dennis Crowley talks about, he noticed that some of his friends were also checked in nearby. They all met at the restaurant, enjoyed dinner, and ran up a large bill, and the customer posted a four-star review. This is the type of customer a restaurant wants to attract. One glance at his Yelp profile shows someone who goes out a lot, spends money, posts reviews and tips, and likes to share recommendations with friends. But he goes to places that are *fun*. On that day Bryant Park Grill gave him something to smile about.

Most restaurants take money in exchange for food. By offering an enticing reward for a simple achievement, Bryant Park Grill stands out in its neighborhood as a place that serves up entertainment along with its daily menu.

CHECKING IN

Foursquare turns life into a game, and games are fun. The English writer G. K. Chesterton once said, "Angels fly because they take themselves lightly." Having a sense of humor is good advice—for life and for your social media efforts.

🔓 UNLOCK THE POWER

- **Find your voice.** NASA's "voice" is about exploration. The content it chooses to share on social media platforms is consistent with its mission. It uses Twitter differently than foursquare, but its voice doesn't change.
- **Broaden your perspective.** Bryant Park Grill launched a unique foursquare campaign because it looked beyond its four walls. Think about your business, product, or service from a broader perspective.

CHAPTER 15

10 Pitfalls to Avoid

> " Sixty-four percent of respondents said that in the past 12 months they had left a store because service was poor. "
>
> —*CONSUMER REPORTS*, July 2011

We have spent the last chapters hearing about best practices from brands, merchants, and businesses around the world, but now it's important to review the problems that might crop up as you create a foursquare strategy or promotion—problems that are easily avoidable. Here are 10 pitfalls that can easily derail your foursquare campaign.

1. Poor Training

No promotion—traditional or digital—stands a chance of success if the people tasked with the administration of the initiative know very little, if anything, about it. Unfortunately, with any new mobile social networking tool, too many marketers put the cart before the horse—or in this case the reward before the training. A friend of mine was excited to see that a local steakhouse was running a foursquare special.

"I see you're on foursquare," my friend excitedly told the server.

"I don't know what that is," the server said. "Let me get my manager."

The restaurant's manager emerged from the kitchen area, greeted my friend with a smile, and asked, "How may I help you?"

"I see that you're on foursquare and that you're offering a special. We'd like to take advantage of it."

"Four what?" asked the manager.

"Never mind," said my friend.

Similar conversations are repeated far too frequently at small and large brands alike.

On one recent weekend I brought my girls to a toy store so they could buy something with their "tooth fairy" money. I noticed the store was running a foursquare special for Lego: buy one and get 50 percent off all Lego City products.

"I see you have a foursquare special for Lego. How's that going?" I asked the clerk who was ringing me up. I could tell by the look on her face that she didn't know a thing about it.

"I'm sorry, I've never heard of that," the clerk said as she shook her head.

Thank goodness my girls didn't want Lego that day. I felt sorry for the poor customer who actually would try to unlock the special when the lines were 30 minutes long on the holiday weekend. That particular clerk would have had to call a manager, leaving the other customers waiting and growing more frustrated by the minute.

Chili's Grill & Bar came up with a simple, creative solution to help its 80,000 employees understand its foursquare special. It added eight words to the foursquare special. When users unlocked the special (free chips and salsa) and showed their phone to the server, it read: Chili's servers, user coupon code #23 to redeem. The odds are good that you have fewer than 80,000 employees to train. If Chili's can do it, so can you.

Go ahead and create a foursquare special, but make sure your staff knows about it.

2. Limited Specials

Chili's inadvertently created an innovative special because it was one of the first chains to offer something for everyone who checked in. In many locations the competition is fierce to become mayor of an establishment, and unless someone is there every single day, they may never become mayor of the venue. But these are still loyal customers, and foursquare offers several types of specials to reward people other than the mayor. Brewerkz in Singapore offers its mayor a free pint of beer once a day, and it offers free fries or onion rings to anyone who checks in and leaves a foursquare tip.

Develop creative ways to engage all your customers in your social media efforts, not just the mayors.

3. Lame Specials

I checked into a winery and was pleasantly surprised that it was offering a special. That is, until I took a closer look at it. The winery was offering 5 percent off my wine purchase on my fifth check-in! I love wine, but I highly doubt I'll be checking into the same tasting room five times in the foreseeable future. And 5 percent does not even take care of the sales tax in California (9.75 percent). To top it off, the employees did not know about it.

If you're going to participate in foursquare and offer specials as an incentive to visit your winery or venue, then make it worthwhile. One restaurant chain offers 10 free chicken wings with every check-in. That's a good special. PYT in Philadelphia offered an open bar to anyone who checked in on a particularly snowy day. It worked too well. The restaurant was packed, and PYT shut off its special. That's OK. If your special works too well, good for you! You can always turn it off or change it.

Create specials that grab my attention.

4. Incongruent Strategy

Make sure your foursquare strategy is aligned with your brand's unique product, service, value, and mission. I came across a dentist's office that was offering free coffee on check-in. It was the oddest thing. Confusing, really. Why would a dentist promote a beverage that stains your teeth? And what does coffee have to do with a dentist? Nothing, really. How about sugar-free candy, instead? Look, I give the dentist credit for trying to be creative, but try to be consistent with your unique value in the community. Odd and confusing specials, promotions, or tips are annoying, turning off your customers instead of attracting them.

Align your foursquare strategy with your business.

5. Failing to Promote Your Participation

You can have the most creative idea on how to engage your mobile customers, but if nobody knows about it, it doesn't matter. The most successful case studies in this book come from individuals and companies that promote their participation with the service.

When McDonald's launched a New York City foursquare campaign in the summer of 2011, its marketing department sent point-of-sales signage to all 621 McDonald's restaurants participating in the event. Arby's, a U.S. restaurant chain specializing in roast beef sandwiches, launched a foursquare promotion where it offered reserved seats for the mayors. It also included 50 percent off meals. Customers who walked into an Arby's restaurant in participating locations saw tabletop brochures that read, "You're at the mayor's seat." It intersected social media conversation with real-world experience. Some restaurants and taverns write the name of the mayor on a blackboard or feature the mayor's name on a large-screen digital display. And of course, the most successful foursquare promotions are heavily publicized on Facebook and Twitter. Leverage other forms of social media to promote your foursquare campaign.

If you join foursquare, tell people about it.

6. Salesy Tips

Some marketing folks at Lionsgate thought they would use foursquare for a guerrilla marketing approach to promote its new movie, *The Expendables*. Marketers left tips at venues such as bars and restaurants. At Five Guys Burgers & Fries in

235

Washington, D.C., a foursquare user might have come across this tip:

> With over 250,000 ways to order your burger it's no wonder that Five Guys burgers are considered bad ass. Brought to you by THE EXPENDABLES opening August 13!

All the tips incorporated "bad ass" and the movie date. As you might imagine, foursquare users complained online that the promotion was a type of spam.

Use foursquare to engage in conversations, not manipulation.

7. Ignoring the Mayor

Mayors take their titles very seriously and there is serious competition for the position in many venues. Treat your mayors like the royalty that they are. The mayors of Luke's Lobster in New York City receive a 10 percent discount. That's not an unusual special, but they also get their photos displayed on wall-mounted TV screens. The mayors literally feel like the real thing when they walk in and are greeted by name. This book is filled with successful case studies of businesses that offer bold incentives to the mayor of their establishment. Extra-special incentives create competition and generate buzz.

Stoke competition among your customers by offering the mayor extra rewards.

8. Stale Specials

Keep your specials updated. Don't just try it once and forget about it. If your customers see that you're offering a special with a lapsed expiration date, it will leave a bad impression about your establishment. A friend of mine was shopping at a popular mall in San Jose, California, on January 5 and found that the mall itself had a good special—the mayor would be rewarded with a $25 gift certificate. Too bad the special was good only through November 12th of the previous year. Nobody had bothered to pull down the special after the date, nor had they kept it up to date.

If you're going to offer a foursquare special, stay on top of it.

9. Poor Customer Service

Customer service is in a sorry state. Most surveys suggest that the majority of customers are frustrated by poor service, and when they're upset they complain online. Unhappy customers are more likely to share negative experiences with their social networks. If your training is inadequate and you are getting a ton of complaints about your service on Yelp, Facebook, Twitter, or other social media sites, please don't attract even more customers to your place. If your leadership or management skills are the problem, foursquare won't solve it.

Offer exceptional customer service before attracting new customers.

(237)

10. Doing It Just to Do It

Many businesses are motivated to join social media out of fear. They're afraid of being left behind, and that's the only reason they do it. They create social media pages and promotions with no clear objective. They do it just to do it. They are joining out of fear instead of joining because they are passionate about engaging their customers. This apathy shows up in the form of lukewarm specials, poor execution, little or no training, and bad customer service.

Get involved with foursquare and mobile social media because you want to engage your customers in a fun, meaningful, and innovative way.

CHAPTER 16

Foursquare Founders in Their Own Words

> *Don't let people tell you that your ideas can't work.*

—**DENNIS CROWLEY,** Cofounder, foursquare

Foursquare founders Naveen Selvadurai and Dennis Crowley

Interview with Dennis Crowley, CEO and Cofounder

Carmine (CG): I understand you went to the S. I. Newhouse School of Communications at Syracuse. I went to Medill at Northwestern. Both are great journalism schools. Did you want to become a journalist?

Dennis Crowley (DC): Yes, I was at the Newhouse School studying journalism from 1994–1998.[1] I used to create newsletters, and I liked the idea of publishing. When I started using a Web browser, I got excited about publishing on the Web. I started with online diaries, recapping my weekend, and telling stories online. I've been doing a blog for 13 years that goes back to my freshman year in college. I used to work on it more when I had more time. It's at www.teendrama. com. But yeah, I went to the Newhouse School for journalism. I was obsessed with magazines, but by the end of college, people started talking about the Internet, so I paid attention. One of my first gigs was working at an ad agency, making websites, and thinking about online campaigns.

CG: It sounds like you were always thinking about creating new experiences.

> **DC:** I had a ton of ideas. I was recently cleaning out my apartment and found an old notebook from a trip to Europe that I had taken with my cousin. In the notebook, there were sketches and notes with ideas like "when you walk by a billboard, they should change to target you" or "the palm pilot should know about the experience you're having or what you like to do, or recommend magazines." It was very real stuff. I always asked questions.

CG: In 2001, you started Dodgeball, which sounds like an early version of foursquare. Google bought it and quashed it. You regrouped and met Naveen Selvadurai, and the two of you started foursquare, launching it at the South by Southwest Festival in March 2009. How are the two services similar?

> **DC:** The common theme is we are building things that change the way you experience the world when you're walking around, whether it's in a random city, mall, or your neighborhood. Dodgeball had the same idea. Both started as tools that make the real world easier and more interesting. It all started with a group of friends asking, "How do we make New York easier to use?" It evolved into "How do you make cities easier to use?" Today, it's "How do you make the world easier to use?"
>
> As I get older, the definition of what makes my life easier changes. Dodgeball was all about how to meet up with friends and go to as many parties as you could in one night. Foursquare has evolved. It's a given that I know where my friends are. Now, it's what to do with the data and how to crowdsource your experience with a city. If I have 20 minutes to kill, what's the best way for me to find information on what I should do? That recommendation will come from a friend of mine.

(241)

CG: I enjoy hearing the story of how a start-up evolves into a successful company. It's interesting that foursquare seems to have evolved beyond its original intention. So let's talk about vision. What was our original vision for foursquare, where is it today, and where will it be two years from now?

> **DC:** Our original vision was to reproduce some of the functionality we lost in Dodgeball. We had these really cool tools that would tell you where your friends were. When we heard that Google was going to turn it off, we had to reproduce it because nobody else was doing it.

It was how we communicated as friends here in New York City. At the same time, I was working at a company producing games. So the next layer was turning life into a game. How do you make a leaderboard or scoreboard for Saturday night? We came up with badges, mayors, and points. We wanted to find out who had more fun or a more diverse life. Naveen added the perspective of including tips and to-dos. Instead of carrying around scraps of paper or articles with names of restaurants that you want to hit, you should carry those on your phone.

So we started with a simple idea—knowing where your friends are. Once we had the location element, we built other things on top of it, like crowdsourced city guide, tips and to-dos, and life as a game.

CG: Has the vision evolved?

DC: We didn't expect the venue stuff. We didn't think about connecting local merchants with customers. That wasn't our goal. It happened organically through foursquare. The venues and merchants figured out that they could use foursquare to their advantage. That was not our idea. It was their idea.

CG: That's fascinating because it's an integral part of the platform. This book is full of stories of how merchants are engaging customers in a deeper way and making more meaningful connections. I'm fascinated to hear that it wasn't part of the plan.

DC: In March 2009, we didn't have a lot of people who wanted to fund us. They would ask, "How do you make money off it?" Nobody knew how the ideas would play out. But once the venues started using it, we created the Merchant Platform and it gave foursquare a kick in the pants. The merchants turned foursquare from an interesting project into an interesting company.

CG: Where do you see it in two years?

DC: The vision doesn't change. Make things that make the world easier for people to explore. But the tools we roll out will continue to change. Nobody has done what we're doing or have tried to tackle these problems. It was groundbreaking two years ago to be able to follow your friends. Now we want you to be able to stand anywhere on the planet, open your phone, and have foursquare tell you something to do nearby. We're taking steps to reach that goal.

Let's take it further. Imagine that your phone wakes up and says, "Hey, Dennis, I know that you're new to this neighborhood. We can tell you that the people who go to the sandwich place you love in New York also happen to love the sandwich place around the corner." It's technology that manufactures serendipity.

CG: Speaking of those serendipitous moments, when you run into friends at the same place, do you have a lot of friends, badges, and mayorships?

DC: I've got about 100 friends. Getting mayorships in New York is tough because it's so competitive. And I've got a lot of badges, but I'm missing the Gym Rat badge.

CG: You're not the only one at foursquare who seems to be missing the Gym Rat badge. You're working too hard.

DC: Yeah, I've been going to the gym more often just to get it!

CG: It sounds like foursquare is trying to keep a limit on the number of badges available.

DC: When we first launched there were only 16. The idea was to make them special, like a Boy Scout or Girl Scout badge. There aren't 100,000 Boy Scout badges. There are 100, and they represent different things. We wanted to keep badges scarce, a special event in the foursquare community. We don't want badges to be tied to specific places. We want them to summarize aggregate experiences like The Wine Bar because you've been to more wine bars than the average person can go to in a lifetime. You got your Coffee badge because you experienced a lot of different coffee shops. We try to stay away from badges tied to one spot, like going to Disneyland. Now if you get a badge for going to every amusement park in the country, that's a cool one. I rode on the 10 craziest roller coasters. That's a good one. We try to make badges around experiences.

CG: So you're saying mayorships are venue specific, badges are experience specific.

DC: That's exactly right. The badges are designed to look like Boy Scout and Girl Scout badges. You earn them by doing different things. If you have to put 100 hours into earning the Boy Scout first-aid badge, we think you should put in 10 or 12 check-ins to earn a badge. For merchants, we want them to claim their venue on foursquare. We've built a robust system that lets them claim their place. Once you claim your venue, you can start running specials. We have great tools that allow

243

for tiered specials and for your best customer, your mayor, anyone who checked in twice this week, and so on. The tools get more robust.

CG: Dennis, how do you respond to a merchant who might have heard about foursquare but says something like, "I have a Facebook page. I have a website. I don't have time for this other stuff."

DC: I would say you are missing a customer feedback channel. You heard the same thing in the early days of Twitter—I have a Facebook page, why should I be on Twitter? But Twitter allows local merchants to interact with customers. You tweet when the cookies come out or when the taco truck moves to a new location. Foursquare also has a fun, playful way of letting you interact with customers. You've been here more than anyone else? You're the mayor. You checked in three times? You get credit for doing it.

I think merchants appreciate the fact that once you claim your venue and we verify it, you get access to all the stats on who's coming to your place and when. If you're a restaurant owner, you have a pretty good idea that you have the biggest crowd at lunch and dinner. But we can show you your best customer or people who used to be your best customer and now are going somewhere else. We have a lot of data. We continue to build tools to give merchants insights. This can potentially drive more traffic.

CG: Dennis, you often use the word *playful* in describing foursquare. Why is the element of play so important?

DC: It should be fun. It turns real life into a game. The point is to make the mundane more playful. People criticized Twitter by asking, why do I care what someone ate for lunch? The foursquare version of that criticism is, why would someone check in at a supermarket or deli? Well, because I get more points, or become the mayor, or unlock a badge. You're taking the mundane parts of your life and making them more playful, fun, and interesting.

Now think about the local merchant. If you're a local merchant, whether you know it or not, people are checking into your place. If you claim your venue and see your stats, we're happy to give those to you. If you want to use data to interact with customers, it will drive business. You don't have to do it, but there's no reason not to do it.

CG: Where does foursquare fit in to the bigger world of mobile social media?

DC: A lot of people see social media brands as competitive (Facebook, Twitter, etc.), but they are actually complementary. Merchants use Twitter to broadcast information, Groupon is a great tool for customer acquisition, and foursquare is great for acquisition and loyalty. The key thing is that we're building tools that merchants have never had access to before. Local merchants have had the Yellow Pages and that's about it. Now there's a whole generation of start-ups making tools for them. If you show the Analytics Dashboard to giant retailers, they will tell you that they have access to some of the data, but not your average mom-and-pop. When you add our tools on top of those stats, that's mind-blowing. We are redefining and reinventing local advertising. Foursquare gives everyday people, venues, and local merchants a voice. It opens the doors for them to see their customers in a new way.

CG: Does foursquare's growth and popularity surprise you?

DC: We're always surprised. We started foursquare so 50 of our friends could follow each other around New York City. I recall sitting in an investment meeting and someone asked, "When are you going to hit one million users?" I said if we ever hit one million users, we've done something right. In one year we hit six million. It's a big surprise.

CG: When was the epiphany moment, the moment you turned to Naveen and said, "This is a lot bigger than we thought it would be."

DC: (laughing) We have one every couple of weeks. I remember when we would be holed up in my apartment and working round the clock at the kitchen table. It was around the time we started the tips—if you check in to a location, you can unlock a message your friend left behind. I remember checking in to a birthday party in a neighborhood and up popped a tip that Naveen had left. I thought to myself—this is going to be so cool. No one has done anything like this!

CG: Why do you have an open API?

DC: We have an open API so people can build something on top of our data set. We have a humble realization that we can't build everything you want. Here are some tools to help you build the things you want. People now build apps on top of our platform. Think about the early days of Twitter. Twitter never made a Twitter client like TweetDeck or Hootsuite. We are seeing the same thing happen with foursquare. We didn't make an Android app. Someone made it for us. We took it in-house to make it better. Someone built the Windows Mobile app, and

245

we improved it. Now you see thousands of developers building every-thing from dating apps to a service where if you check in to a restaurant that has a lousy health inspection, you'll see a text message that tells you to get out. That's not stuff we anticipated when we sat around the kitchen table.

CG: Finally, let's talk about entrepreneurship. I love this quote I heard from you: "Don't let people tell you your ideas won't work." Did you encounter skeptics?

DC: Sure. I remember when I built an early version of Dodgeball and my boss at the time told me, "People don't care about reviews that other people write. They want to read reviews that experts write." I don't think that's true. Then I heard, "Nobody is ever going to remember to take their phone out of their pocket to check in." I bet they would. Then I heard, "Life as a game—that's a stupid idea. Nobody wants make-believe badges." I thought they would.

But you're missing the second sentence of my quote. "If they do tell you it won't work, at least prove it to yourself by making and testing a prototype." Maybe the idea isn't as good as you thought it would be. Then you can refine and tweak it. Foursquare is one big open experiment.

Can I tell you about one more thing we're really proud of?

CG: By all means. Go for it.

DC: We have about 50 employees, and nobody is making cold calls. Every company that I've worked at has a floor of people making calls. We don't have it. We've turned our users into a passionate community. Merchants hear about specials and mayors not by us, but by our users. We always hear stories about users who introduce the service to local merchants. We also hear, "I'm the mayor, what do I get?" If that happens enough, merchants start asking questions. That's how it has taken off. Users are pitching the venues to create specials. I've never seen any company pull it off. Our superusers are a crowdsourced version of a sales force.

CG: Yes, that is unusual. It has been a pleasure to feature your company and its users. I hope you're looking forward to a book on it.

DC: We're psyched!

Interview with Naveen Selvadurai, Head of Platform and Cofounder

CG: Naveen, give me a sense of how foursquare came to be.

Naveen Selvadurai (NS): Both Dennis and I had been kicking around ideas in this space for a couple of years.[2] We really wanted to build something great on mobile. We wanted to build something that would help us explore our city and connect with friends. Dennis lived in the East Village, and I lived in SoHo. You always read about these amazing things to do in New York City, and we wanted an easier way to keep track of them and share these experiences with our friends.

CG: How did you and Dennis get to know each other?

NS: We both had quit our previous jobs [Naveen had left Sony and Dennis had left Google] around the same time, and we started working independently in a shared office space in New York's Union Square. This was in May 2007. Although we worked on different projects, they were all related to the mobile and game space. We became friends, and over the next year we realized that we were working on similar ideas. We started bringing our concepts together in late 2008. In January 2009 we knew South by Southwest was coming up in March, and we thought it would be a good time to launch the platform we had been working on—foursquare.

CG: You grew to one million users in your first year, and by your second anniversary you had about seven million users. That's astonishing growth. Faster than Twitter at similar stages. Are you at all surprised?

NS: It always continues to surprise and amaze us. We are constantly surprised by what partners are doing and how users are extending the platform in ways that we never expected. We grew 3,400 percent in 2010. We saw 380 million check-ins around the world. We're getting 2 million check-ins a day and at least one check-in from every country in the world. We plotted the check-ins on a map. We literally had a check-in on every major continent and even on tiny islands in the middle of the ocean. We're still a small company. Foursquare was only Dennis and I for the first year. By January 2010, we had grown to 7 people. Today we're at 50. Today we also have 2,000 developers on our API. They are

247

building or thinking about applications on top of our API. It's all very incredible.

Carmine, do you know what we're really passionate about?

CG: What's that, Naveen?

NS: Our users. They have taken up the cause on so many levels. Remember I told you the first year it was just me and Dennis. We did everything—coding, PR, marketing. The users stepped up. They would give us badge ideas. Superusers would help us answer questions on the user forum. There aren't too many services where users have that kind of passion. They promote us on Twitter and Facebook. For the first year we tried to answer every question, every tweet because we wanted our users to know that we were building this for them.

So if you ask what really surprises me, I would say the passion of our users. They hold meet-ups on their own. Users take it upon themselves to have an event in a city to unlock a badge. In April 2010, some users said April 16 is really cool because 4 squared equals 16. We called it foursquare Day. Users came together all around the world—there were parties in 80 cities! Even the mayor of Manchester, New Hampshire, declared it foursquare Day.

CG: I was impressed with the stories I heard from businesses, merchants, and the users themselves. Everyone seems to have a different reason to use foursquare.

NS: They sure do. I know one student who says he goes to class to retain his mayorship. One girl who is a superfan also is the mayor of Chelsea Piers, a popular gym on the west side of New York City. And she has held it for more than one year. No one can unseat her. She's very proud of it.

CG: Naveen, has the vision changed at all from the days when you and Dennis shared your small office space?

NS: We are still building on a lot of the core ideas. We started the service in a playful way—to make cities easier to explore. For example, think about the concept of a to-do list that you carry around in your pocket. Before foursquare, I would rip things out of a magazine with ideas of things I wanted to do in the city. Well, we are still working on these core ideas for our foursquare users. Everyone—young and old— can fall in love with the idea of a to-do list. At its core, foursquare gets people to explore, try new things, compete with friends, and share with friends. That's the core vision and will continue to drive us forward.

CG: Let's talk about game mechanics. The idea of earning points, badges, mayorships. This is critical for foursquare's success. Was this part of the original vision?

NS: Given what we learned from previous projects, we wanted to apply a layer of game theory to foursquare. The question we asked was, "How can we use software to change behavior. How can we make it more playful for people to explore their world?"

CG: There's that *playful* word again. Dennis says the same thing.

NS: It's true. Foursquare gets you off your couch or your computer and encourages you to explore your world. Many other social networks are about being behind your computer screen or TV. But why not get out and try the new bar or the new place for lunch?

We came up with the idea of mayor. Wouldn't it be cool to reward the most loyal person in a bar or restaurant? This concept of recognizing loyal patrons goes back hundreds of years. We like to go to places where they know our name. We like free stuff when we walk into the door. And since everyone respects the mayor, we're giving you the opportunity to earn the honorary title. This creates competition. People want to prove their loyalty to a business and to their friends so they check in more often.

For example, how do you earn the Pizzaiola badge? You have to visit 20 different pizza places. Too often we go back to the same pizza place. But in New York City, why don't you try something different and get to know the city better? The game exists to encourage you to complete your city. Think of your city as a game board. For example, are you a real New Yorker if you haven't been to each of the five boroughs? What if we made a badge to encourage that? People would try to earn the badge.

CG: Is that really a badge?

NS: No, but it's a good idea! This is how we think of life as a game.

CG: Let's talk about businesses—small and large. What's in it for them?

NS: One, the users are really passionate about the service. The reason specials got in the system was because our users started hassling bartenders and waitresses to do something interesting to reward them. Even in the early days, May 2009, restaurants would advertise that they give mayors a free drink. Businesses were doing it before we even added the function to foursquare. Users are leading the way, and they are your customers. This is unique to foursquare. Users visit your place and talk about it with their friends in a way that's fun and playful.

CG: Why do you think your users are so passionate? They really are crazy about it.

NS: It's fun. It's easy to show off your achievements to your friends. It's very easy to share your favorite place. The badges, points, and mayorships make users minicelebrities. A bartender may know your name. When you're the mayor you might be the coolest person in the room for five minutes. Who doesn't want recognition? And on top of it, you're rewarding my loyalty.

CG: Do you have any mayorships or badges you're proud of?

NS: I'm the mayor of a Spanish grocery store in my neighborhood, but I'll lose it soon. New York is pretty competitive. My favorite badge is Brooklyn for Life, which you get for 25 check-ins in Brooklyn. It shows that I get out there. I haven't been to a gym in a long time, so I want to unlock the Gym Rat badge.

CG: Here we go again with the Gym Rat badge. You're the third person I've talked to at foursquare who wants to unlock the badge. I told the others you guys are working too hard.

NS: It's crazy busy, definitely.

CG: What was it like to be named by World Economic Forum as a tech pioneer for 2011?

NS: We were totally surprised. We are constantly excited by everything we see.

CG: Thanks, Naveen. Congratulations on your success.

NS: Thank you. It's great to see someone outside of our industry writing about us and making it simple to understand.

Conclusion

Your Turn to Check In

I hope these stories inspire you to think differently about your business and what foursquare might mean to your success. Now it's your turn to check in and try it for yourself. A revolution is happening, and you need to be part of it. "Social, location-based mobile commerce is revolutionizing the way we shop and engage with businesses,"[1] says Sumeet Jain, a venture capitalist with CMEA Capital who has traveled to 30 countries in search of emerging technologies. Jain told me he's a big believer in the power of foursquare primarily for the data it provides merchants. "For the first time businesses have an enormous wealth of actionable information: who their best customers are, when they are at your business, when they've been to your business, and when they are likely to come again. This will empower business owners to interact and engage with their customers in ways they've never been able to do. It's a powerful way to find new customers, engage existing customers, and help your existing customers find even more customers."

As more business and commerce activities shift to the mobile phone, you'll want to make sure your business is there. Companies are experimenting with near-field communications (NFC) technologies that make it possible for you to pay for things like gas, food, or clothes with a tap of your phone. Commerce is going mobile and you'll want to be where people are living their lives and doing business. American Express is in partnership with foursquare to create a unique system whereby AmEx customers can register their cards in the foursquare system to get access to special offers from participating merchants. According to the *Wall Street Journal*, "AmEx is racing to attract tech-savvy customers who in the future will make purchases through their mobile phones."[2] AmEx is going to where its customers are, and its customers are increasingly on foursquare.

As I was writing this book, I dropped into a local coffee shop, and on my way out I started talking to a franchise owner whom I've come to know. We greeted each other, and he asked me about my new project. Although he seemed intrigued, he ended the conversation with these words: "I'm usually too busy to think about these social media things." Here's the twist. This particular franchise owner was reading a 500-page textbook and had filled an entire yellow legal pad with notes. "What are you studying?" I asked him. "I'm taking a test to get a contractor's license," he said. That's all I needed to know. You see, this franchise owner had plenty of time to study for a very difficult license that was not core to his business, but he had no time to learn social media—even though setting up a foursquare account and creating the first special can take as little as 30 minutes.

If you are genuinely committed to moving your brand forward, rewarding loyal customers, and offering your customers and clients an experience to remember, you will find time to learn more about the new tools now available to you. If not, it's perfectly OK . . . with your competitors. They'll love you for it.

If you're not committed to learning about new tools to engage your customers, perhaps running a business isn't for you. Maybe you're not cut out for creating a business that offers innovative products, services, and experiences. When Steve Jobs was asked why the Apple stores became hugely successful when other computer stores had failed, he said the other stores were in the business of "moving boxes." Instead Apple was in the business of "enriching lives." Mobile location-based services will help you enrich the lives of your customers, and they will reward you for it.

The social, local, and mobile space is changing and growing every day. Statistics and examples in this book will change, but the principles required for successful mobile marketing campaigns will remain relevant. However, I do urge you to keep up with news and inspiring ideas in the following resources:

- the official foursquare blog: http://blog.foursquare.com
- foursquare community: http://aboutfoursquare.com
- Dennis Crowley's Twitter posts: @DENS
- Naveen Selvadurai's Twitter posts: @naveen
- Carmine's Twitter posts: @carminegallo
- Carmine's foursquare page: http://foursquare.com/ carminegallo
- the Power of foursquare website: http://poweroffoursquare .com

An influential acting teacher once said, "Overcome the notion that you must be regular. It robs you of the chance to be extraordinary." If you've decided to run or manage a business, don't settle for mediocrity. In today's competitive global economy, it's not enough to be average. Average only guarantees below-average results. Set yourself apart. Be extraordinary. Get social. Go mobile. Enjoy the ride!

Notes

INTRODUCTION

1. Dennis Crowley, CEO and cofounder, foursquare, in discussion with the author, January 26, 2011.

CHAPTER 1

1. Matthew Shadbolt, director of Internet marketing, The Corcoran Group, in discussion with the author, January 20, 2011.
2. Ibid.
3. Naveen Selvadurai, head of platform and cofounder, foursquare, in discussion with the author, January 24, 2011.
4. *China Daily*, "China Daily in Partnership with Foursquare: Love China, Explore China," http://foursquare.com/chinadailyusa (accessed March 29, 2011).
5. Chris Thompson, blogger, http://aboutfoursquare.com, in discussion with the author, January 26, 2011.
6. *China Daily*, "China Daily in Partnership with Foursquare."

CHAPTER 2

1. Maria Avgitidis, founder, Agape Match, in discussion with the author, January 12, 2011.
2. Wendy Harman, social media director, American Red Cross, in discussion with the author, January 28, 2011.

CHAPTER 3

1. Dennis Crowley, CEO and cofounder, foursquare, in discussion with the author, January 26, 2011.
2. Jo Stratmann, marketing manager, FreshNetworks, in discussion with the author, February 1, 2011.
3. Tristan Walker, vice president of business development, foursquare, in discussion with the author, January 17, 2011.
4. Nate Bonilla-Warford, Dr., founder of foursquare Day, in discussion with the author, February 2, 2011.

CHAPTER 4

1. Nicole Cochran, marketing director, Chili's Grill & Bar, in discussion with the author, January 26, 2011.
2. Ray Wan, marketing manager, Earthjustice, in discussion with the author, December 28, 2010.

CHAPTER 5

1. Christina Sponselli, social media director, University of California–Berkeley, in discussion with the author, January 12, 2011.
2. BART news article, "BART/Foursquare Survey: 38% Say Foursquare Makes Riding BART 'More Fun'," May 5, 2010, www.bart.gov/news/articles/2010/news20100505.aspx (accessed February 13, 2011).
3. Richard Bonds, director of social media, the Pennsylvania Office of Tourism, in discussion with the author, January 13, 2011.

CHAPTER 6

1. Adam Wallace, digital media director, Roger Smith Hotel, in discussion with the author, January 11, 2011.
2. Angel Aristone, director of communications and social media, Six Flags, in discussion with the author, January 26, 2011.

CHAPTER 7

1. B. J. Emerson, vice president of technology, Tasti D-Lite, in discussion with the author, January 7, 2011.
2. Tristan Walker, vice president of business development, foursquare, in discussion with the author, January 17, 2011.
3. David Meyers, aka Spam, foursquare superuser, in discussion with the author, March 22, 2011.

CHAPTER 8

1. Eddie Dopkin, owner of Miss Shirley's Cafe, in discussion with the author, January 28, 2011.
2. Ryan Goff, director of social media marketing, MGH Baltimore, in discussion with the author regarding Miss Shirley's Cafe foursquare special, January 28, 2011.
3. Lori Levine Ordover, managing member of the Ordover Group, in discussion with the author, March 16, 2011.

CHAPTER 9

1. Joe Sorge, owner, AJ Bombers, in discussion with the author, January 24, 2011.
2. Matt Murphy and Mary Meeker, "Top Mobile Internet Trends," Slideshare.net, February 10, 2011, www.slideshare.net/kleiner perkins/kpcb-top-10-mobile-trends-feb-2011 (accessed March 21, 2011).
3. Ibid.
4. Business News Daily Staff, "Social Media Now Top Marketing Pick for Local Businesses," *Business News Daily* online, February 21, 2011, www.businessnewsdaily.com/social-media-now-top -marketing-pick-for-local-businesses-1016 (accessed March 21, 2011).
5. News release, "New Research Finds that Customer Loyalty Programs Help Restaurants Weather the Economy, Gain Competitive Edge," National Restaurant Association, August 10, 2010, www.restaurant.org/pressroom/pressrelease/?ID=1988 (accessed March 21, 2011).
6. Chad Pollitt, "Why Your Business Should Take Foursquare and Geosocial Media Seriously," Business 2 Community, February 27, 2011, www.b2cmarketinginsider.com/online-marketing/ why-your-business-should-take-foursquare-geosocial-media -seriously-016646 (accessed March 21, 2011).
7. Jeff Bussgang, "Why Did Foursquare Succeed Where Other Location-Based Services Failed?," Businessinsider.com, March 2, 2011, www.businessinsider.com/figuring-out-foursquare -2011-3 (accessed March 21, 2011).
8. Erick Schonfeld, "[Founder Stories] Foursquare's Dennis Crowley: 'Stop Sketching, Start Building,'" March 5, 2011, http:// techcrunch.com/2011/03/05/founder-stories-foursquare-crow ley-stop-sketching-start-building/ (accessed March 21, 2011).
9. Ibid.
10. Business News Daily Staff, "Social Media Now Top Marketing Pick for Local Businesses," *Business News Daily* online, February 21, 2011, www.businessnewsdaily.com/social-media-now-top -marketing-pick-for-local-businesses-1016 (accessed March 21, 2011).

CHAPTER 10

1. Matt Rodbard, social media manager, Metromix, in discussion with the author, January 14, 2011.

CHAPTER 11

1. Sassy Thomas, superuser, foursquare, in discussion with the author, February 2, 2011.
2. Lee Applbaum, CMO, RadioShack, in discussion with the author, February 2, 2011.
3. Dennis Crowley, CEO and cofounder, foursquare, in discussion with the author, January 26, 2011.
4. Chris Anderson, *Free: How Today's Smartest Businesses Profit by Giving Something for Nothing* (New York: Hyperion, 2009), p. 10.

CHAPTER 12

1. Tracy Marks, public relations/social media specialist, Souplantation & Sweet Tomatoes, in discussion with the author, December 3, 2010.
2. Jonathan Fornaci, president and CEO, Straw Hat Restaurants, in discussion with the author, March 14, 2011.

CHAPTER 13

1. Ellen Stone, vice president of marketing, Bravo, in discussion with the author, December 30, 2011.

CHAPTER 14

1. Stephanie Schierholz, social media manager, NASA, in discussion with the author, March 13, 2011.

CHAPTER 16

1. Dennis Crowley, CEO and cofounder, foursquare, in discussion with the author, January 26, 2011.
2. Naveen Selvadurai, head of platform and cofounder, foursquare, in discussion with the author, January 24, 2011.

CONCLUSION

1. Sumeet Jain, partner, CMEA Capital, in discussion with the author, March 16, 2011.
2. Shayndi Raice and Robin Sidel, "AmEx Teams Up with Foursquare," *Wall Street Journal* online, March 4, 2011, http://online.wsj.com/article/SB1000142405274870407680457618084172 7743146.html (accessed March 29, 2011).

Index

263

264